Cambridge El

Elements in Religion and M
edited by
Chad Meister
Bethel University
Paul K. Moser
Loyola University Chicago

FREUD'S MONOTHEISM

William B. Parsons
Rice University

Shaftesbury Road, Cambridge CB2 8EA, United Kingdom

One Liberty Plaza, 20th Floor, New York, NY 10006, USA

477 Williamstown Road, Port Melbourne, VIC 3207, Australia

314–321, 3rd Floor, Plot 3, Splendor Forum, Jasola District Centre, New Delhi – 110025, India

103 Penang Road, #05–06/07, Visioncrest Commercial, Singapore 238467

Cambridge University Press is part of Cambridge University Press & Assessment, a department of the University of Cambridge.

We share the University's mission to contribute to society through the pursuit of education, learning and research at the highest international levels of excellence.

www.cambridge.org
Information on this title: www.cambridge.org/9781108826518

DOI: 10.1017/9781108919975

First published 2023

A catalogue record for this publication is available from the British Library.

ISBN 978-1-108-82651-8 Paperback
ISSN 2631-3014 (online)
ISSN 2631-3006 (print)

Freud's Monotheism

Elements in Religion and Monotheism

DOI: 10.1017/9781108919975
First published online: January 2023

William B. Parsons
Rice University

Author for correspondence: William B. Parsons, pars@rice.edu

Abstract: This Element consists of three interrelated sections. "What Freud Said" summarizes the salient details of Freud's psychology of religion: his views on the origins and development of Western religions, on contemporary Western monotheisms, on the "unpsychological" proceedings of the religio-cultural superego, his qualified endorsement of religious forms of psychotherapy and his cursory analysis of Eastern religions. "What Freud Got Wrong" surveys the history of the multidisciplinary critiques (anthropological, sociological and, later, psychoanalytic, theological/philosophical) leveled at Freud's interpretative strategies. "Toward a Revised Psychoanalytic Theory of Religion" suggests the best way forward is to employ a psychoanalytic theory of religion that, taking its cue from the history of its critique, houses reflective, inclusive and dialogical elements. It presents illustrations taken from a variety of contemporary religio-cultural phenomena (Marvel movies, issues concerning religion, sexuality and gender, the megachurch and QAnon) as portable lessons for such applications.

Keywords: Freud, psychoanalysis, religion, monotheism, method

ISBNs: 9781108826518 (PB), 9781108919975 (OC)
ISSNs: 2631-3014 (online), 2631-3006 (print)

Contents

1 What Freud Said

Freud's monotheism. What is one to make of this phrase? In university departments of religion, which by definition are not religious social spaces but secular, pluralistic, interdisciplinary and critical, one might present monotheism dispassionately to a waiting student population in terms of how religious traditions express it through their ideologies, practices and institutional accouterments. At the same time one might also offer diverse methods (e.g., humanistic, scientific, social scientific) that have chimed in as to the "what" of monotheism. It is to the latter group that Freud belongs. His psychoanalytic theorizing developed a model of the human personality that became the conceptual framework through which he discerned the empirical reality behind what religions have framed as the divine entity at the core of self, society and universe. In the three major sections that comprise this Element we will look at what Freud said about monotheism and religion in general, the critiques leveled at him and in what qualified sense, despite such critiques, we can still find the application of his theories useful.[1]

1.1 Methods and Religion

Freud was not the first or only social scientist in the late nineteenth and twentieth centuries to take on the formidable task of trying to theorize about the origins of religion. Interestingly enough, he was also not the first or only to look to totemism as the key to such origins. For example, in his book *The Elementary Forms of Religious Life*, Freud's contemporary, the sociologist Emile Durkheim, by way of choosing totemic society as an early, simple form of religion in which the foundational elements were more easily deciphered, argued that religion is a function of group processes. The definitional strategy he promoted was sociological and it ran as follows: religion is a "unified system of beliefs and practices relative to sacred things, that is to say, things set apart and forbidden – beliefs and practices which unite into one single moral community called a Church, all those who adhere to them."[2] For Durkheim religion was not a projection of the individual but of the entire group. The myths and symbols of religion expressed group sentiments and functioned to establish group identity and solidarity. In this sense religion was "eternal": anytime you had a group you would find symbols, myths, things set off as "sacred" and any other religious

---

[1] Throughout this Element I take from or summarize the more detailed commentary found in my *Freud and Religion: Advancing the Dialogue* (Cambridge: Cambridge University Press, 2021). In the latter the interested reader will find an expansion of many of the arguments presented here as well as additional ones relevant to post-Freudian psychoanalytic studies of religion.

[2] E. Durkheim, *The Elementary Forms of Religious Life* (New York: Free Press, 1965[1912]), p. 62.

accouterments, all representations of the group, whose members did not necessarily clothe themselves in the more familiar garb of modern institutional monotheisms. For Durkheim, then, *any* group, from sports teams to universities to political parties (and note that many groups are represented by "totems" like eagles, elephants, donkeys, bears, owls and so on), function like what we today, in restricting religion to institutional religion, think operates. Even countries like the United States function like a religion (the oft-used term "civil religion" applies here). To wit: it has its founders and saints (e.g., presidents and moral leaders), scriptures (the Constitution and Bill of Rights), law and ethics (e.g., SCOTUS), the sacred spaces of buildings and monuments (the White House and Statue of Liberty), symbols (the eagle and flag), sacred days (July 4 and Memorial Day) and rituals (Pledge of Allegiance and juror oaths).

For Durkheim myths, symbols and collective representations were initially engendered through rituals and what he called "collective effervescence." The religious products of the latter then had a claim on us insofar as they were inwardly felt to be above us, just as today we might think of the inward obligations foisted on us by the doctrines of institutional religion. However, for Durkheim this was not due to their ontological status, as theologians might posit. Rather, they were due to the fact that we, as human beings, are what Durkheim called *homo duplex*: we are literally singular and collective (social) human beings at the same time. To nail this down Durkheim took on William James who, in his *The Varieties of Religious Experience*, had defined religion as "the feelings, acts, and experiences of individual men in their solitude, so far as they apprehend themselves to stand in relation to whatever they may consider the divine," further isolating its deepest core in mystical experience.[3] But whereas James found the feeling of ecstasy and otherness in the farther side of the subconscious, Durkheim found it in *homo duplex*, collective effervescence and group functioning. Durkheim's definitional strategy, then, can be framed as offering a sociological version of James' more psycho-spiritual and individualistic theory.

Freud read both Durkheim and James, offering a direct response to the former in his work *Totem and Taboo* and an indirect response to the latter through the figure of Romain Rolland and his "oceanic feeling" (and one could add here Jung as well, which we will attend to shortly). Correspondingly, he also offered a more restrictive definitional strategy when it came to the "what" of religion (which again we will address later in this section). Attending to only Durkheim for now, Freud offered a different view of totemism by locating it historically

---

[3] W. James, *The Varieties of Religious Experience* (New York: Modern Library, 1929[1902]), pp. 31–32.

(through what he called the "primal deed") and developmentally (by which he meant through the generating power of oedipal conflict). In order to make his argument clear, we must take a brief detour through his understanding of the human personality. While Freud's view of the person changed as new clinical data sets emerged from his psychoanalytic practice, we can focus on two components, the structural model and libido theory (i.e., the developmental line of sexuality), that served as the basis for his interpretation of monotheism.

1.2 Freud's Theory of the Personality

As concerns the development of the personality Freud is always linked to his famous Oedipus complex. In turn, the latter is situated in a developmental process known as *libido theory*.

Freud thought that mature forms of object-love had precursors, which is to say "a developmental infrastructure," in the life of children. This developmental line was theorized as consisting in stages, each with its particular "erotogenic" zone. For example, for the first year of life or so, dubbed the "oral phase" of development, sexual development had for its erotogenic zone the mouth, which took pleasure in receiving nurturance from the mother's breast. Next was the anal stage, in which the child learns to defecate on his/her own, the erotogenic zone being the anus. The phallic stage (the erotogenic zone being the genitals) followed and, after a latency period, puberty, where the emerging adolescent takes an object (a person) as its focus of desire. He was also impressed that during the course of development the male child is subject to the vicissitudes of the famous Oedipus complex. In its pure form this means that, on one hand, the male child idealizes and identifies with his father, seeking his protection, admiring his power and wanting his love. On the other hand, the male child also sees the father as the major competitor for his first true love, the mother, and so the feelings of competition, fear (especially of castration), jealousy and guilt (for wishing his death) are also part of and in direct conflict with his feelings of love and identification. Freud's clinical data led him to think that a person might, depending on various life events, become fixated at a particular developmental stage (which, in its extreme form, can lead to sexual perversions). The best outcome would be if the male child identifies with and loves his father more than he hates him and renounces his love of the mother by "displacing" that affection onto a suitable substitute.[4]

---

[4] Freud's major and early statement on the development of sexuality is his *Three Essays on Sexuality*, in *The Standard Edition of the Complete Psychological Works of Sigmund Freud.* 24 vols. Trans. and ed. by J. Strachey. London: Hogarth Press (hereafter referred to as S. E.), vol. 7, pp. 125–145. A brief and readable history of Freud's evolving theory of the instincts can be found

Going on, and as we will detail in the next section, there have been some forceful critiques of the way in which Freud frames the developmental line of females. To be sure, the latter was not simply Oedipus reversed ("Electra complex" was a term coined by Jung and firmly rejected by Freud as developmentally inaccurate). Rather, Freud thought that the developmental trajectory of girls was more complicated. Like little boys, little girls initially identified as "little men" in the oral phase of libidinal development. Like little boys, then, their first love object was the mother. However, by the time girls arrived at the phallic phase, the developmental line took a new turn. Seeing that they did not have a valued appendage that was part of the male anatomy, girls felt castrated, a psychic scar that created "penis envy." The developmental challenge was thus far greater: the girl had to change her love object from the mother to the father and erotogenic zone from clitoris to vagina. Along the way, she would try to actualize her desire for a baby boy (and hence gain her "penis"), evincing the character traits of jealousy, envy, body narcissism, castration shame (Freud thought this was the psychological origin of the social institution of "weaving") and perhaps even a professorship (a good cultural outcome for the sublimation of penis envy). Women were seen as less individuated, more narcissistic and lacking in a sense of justice (which is to say they had a deficient superego), a logic that follows from the psychological reality of having been castrated (the latter obviates any strong need to follow the dictates of the superego, the latter being more effective for men due to the fear of castration).[5]

Things become even more complicated when the developmental line of sexuality is run through Freud's "structural model." The foundational base of the latter is Freud's notion of the unconscious (later referred to as the id). Unlike James' notion of the *sub*conscious and Jung's notion of the *collective* unconscious, Freud insisted on a somatic (biological) dimension of the *un*conscious. Freud isolated two instinctual processes, sex and aggression (later Eros [sexuality and, more widely, the drive for ever greater and more complex forms of unity] and Thanatos [aggression and the eventual quiescence of death]), which served as its biological drivers [Freud's original German term for instinct was *triebe*, best translated as "drive"]). Further, he characterized the unconscious as not so much immoral but amoral: it is ruled by the "pleasure principle," which is to say that instincts seek satisfaction. At our biological core, then, we are

in E. Bibring, "The Development and Problems of the Theory of the Instincts." *International Journal of Psychoanalysis* 22 (1941), 102–131.

[5] To be sure, one finds no dearth of criticism as to Freud's views on female sexuality and development. His own views are best expressed in his later essay titled "Femininity" in his *New Introductory Lectures on Psychoanalysis* (S. E., vol. 22, pp. 112–135). A good overview of the critiques leveled at him can be found in J. Mitchell, *Psychoanalysis and Feminism* (New York: Basic Books, 2nd edition [revised], 2000 [1974]).

animalistic and selfish. The id seeks expression and the "mental" correlate of that somatically based desire is manifested in wishes and fantasies.

If the unconscious is rooted in biological processes, being driven to satisfaction, yet also amoral (with some of the instinctual wishes being socially unacceptable), then there must be a mental function that exists to mediate between such transgressive wishes and a social reality that all too often demands their renunciation. Here is where Freud's notions of the ego (or *Ich*, the felt sense of "I") and superego (the *über-Ich* or "over-I") become important. As opposed to the id, Freud framed the ego as ruled by the "reality-principle" and "secondary-process" thought (i.e., our reason). It helps the id get what it wants but, because it is informed about the social world, it does so in a manner that mitigates and redirects the raw "want" of the id. The ego counters the id through a variety of "defense mechanisms," the most profitable of which are *repression* (the renunciation of the id's wants to the extent possible and in accordance with social mores), *projection* (where one denies one's own impulses and vulnerabilities by projecting them onto other individuals and groups) and *sublimation* (a moral concept that redirects the desires of the id to socially productive pursuits). The extension of the ego to the superego, which is experienced as that moral voice "above" us, happens in a developmental sense through identification with and internalization of the mores of the parental unit (who, it should be noted, are also informed by the mores of the culture "behind" them). The superego internalizes (and is felt subjectively) as the moral rules by which one should abide (the abrogation of which is felt as guilt). These two component parts (ego, superego) of Freud's structural model, then, ensure (ideally at least) that the successful individual can exist in a group "with others" in a way that navigates his/her own preferences with those of others with an eye toward contributing to the common good.

Summing up, then, Freud's model of the way the mind works is a *conflict model*: we are ambivalent beings whose desires will not always jibe with our internalized moral standards. Because unconscious desires are powerful and cannot be entirely repressed, contained or sublimated, they are bound to leak through in some fashion: in dreams, in symptomatic acts, in slips of the tongue, in neurotic symptoms and in all forms of religion.

1.3 The Origins of Religion

Turning now to the application of Freud's model, we have noted that in his era a number of social scientists were interested in theorizing about the origins of religion. Initially what interested Freud the most were anthropological findings about totemism. Freud agreed that totemism was the earliest universal "pre-religious" (relative to the institutional sense) phase of cultural development.

Additionally, he adopted the following from his anthropological colleagues: the totem is a class of assorted material objects (usually animal) that are revered and worshipped; it is understood to be the ancestor and father of the clan who protected the clan and with whom the members of the clan identified (often through dressing up in the guise of the totem); it is not to be killed (except on those few sacred occasions dubbed the "totem meal" when it is permissible in a ceremony to kill the totem and eat it). While the latter characterizes its religious dimension Freud, again relying on his anthropological colleagues, appends to that its social dimension, consisting of a set of laws or "taboos" of which exogamy (the taboo against incest) was primary. Like Durkheim, Freud thought totemism, understood as a pre-religious form, might provide clues as to the nature of later, more developed institutional religion in general (to which he would return in his 1927 work *The Future of an Illusion*).[6] Unlike Durkheim, however, Freud emphasized the determinants of his libido theory, with its emphasis on Oedipus, the latter complicated by the vicissitudes of the structural model.

Given this, it is understandable that Freud, who was convinced of the universality of his theory, would rely on a series of case histories to make his argument. During the course of his narrative in *Totem and Taboo* Freud thought it particularly appropriate to draw our attention to psychoanalytic studies that dealt with analyses of children and their animal phobias. In 1909, just before the writing of *Totem and Taboo*, Freud had written a case history on "little Hans" and his horse phobia.[7] Citing similar psychoanalytic case histories from his colleagues, he concluded that the spectrum of behavior exhibited by children toward animals of various kinds (ranging from simple fear to more complex, conflicted attitudes) are traceable back to the child's father. In psychoanalytic terminology, the child "displaced" the range of emotions and conflicted attitudes found in the Oedipus complex from the father to the totem animal. If human nature is universal, then the real clue to what the totem really is and how it came to be has been found: the totem is nothing but a substitute father. It is in Oedipus, then, that Freud finds the key to the origin of religion.

Freud sought to supplement the findings of his social scientific colleagues by applying the interpretative lens of his depth psychoanalytic approach to explain how totemism came to be. In so doing, he once again adopted select findings of his scholarly colleagues: Darwin's assertion that before the existence of any society there were roving groups of primal men consisting of a feared and envied primal father, his wife (or wives) and sons, some of whom were castrated

---

[6] Here Freud was following in the footsteps of his sociological counterpart E. Durkheim, who employed a similar strategy in his *The Elementary Forms of Religious Life*.

[7] See Freud, S. E., vol. 9, pp. 3–152.

or driven out by the fearsome father; J. J. Atkinson's theory that the primal horde came to an end when the brothers banded together and killed the primal father out of jealousy, competition and envy; and Robertson Smith's suggestion that totemism, now conceived of as a kind of "brother clan," was punctuated by ceremonies in which prohibitions were lifted and the totemic animal was killed and eaten ("the totem meal"). Insisting that the explanation for the origin of totemism needed to be at once "an historical and psychological one," and that it "should tell us under what conditions this peculiar institution developed and to what psychic needs in men it has given expression," Freud then presents his psychoanalytic version of the origin of totemism, beginning with the "acting out" of the oedipal wish to kill the father:[8]

> One day the brothers who had been driven out came together, killed and devoured their father and so made an end of the patriarchal horde. United, they had the courage to do and succeeded in doing what would have been impossible for them individually ... The violent primal father had doubtless been the feared and envied model of each one of the company of brothers and in the act of devouring him they accomplished their identification with him, and each one of them acquired a portion of his strength. The totem meal, which is perhaps mankind's earliest festival, would thus be a repetition and a commemoration of this memorable and criminal deed.[9]

For Freud, then, it was the repeated murder of the primal father that constituted the empirical, historical events (later mythologized in Western, monotheistic scripture) that gave rise to the feeling (as well as to the doctrine) of what scripture and theology narrate as the "original sin" lurking in us all.[10] Moreover, since psychoanalysis claims that the acting out of the hostility toward the father results in guilt and remorse, the invention of that socioreligious institution known as totemism is a kind of memory or cultural monument born of remorse for the great deed:

> Totemic religion arose from the filial sense of guilt[11] ... They thus created out of their filial sense of guilt the two fundamental taboos of totemism, which for that very reason inevitably corresponded to the two repressed wishes of the Oedipus complex[12] ... The totemic system was, as it were, a covenant with their father, in which he promised them everything that a childish imagination may expect from a father – protection, care, and indulgence – while on their side they undertook to respect his life[13] ... society was now based on complicity in the common crime; religion was based on the sense of guilt and the remorse attaching to it; while morality was based partly on the exigencies of this society and partly on the penance demanded by the sense of guilt.[14]

---

[8] Freud, *Totem and Taboo*, S. E., vol. 13, p. 108.   [9] Ibid., pp. 141–142.   [10] Ibid., p. 161.
[11] Ibid., p. 145.   [12] Ibid., p. 143.   [13] Ibid., p. 144.   [14] Ibid., p. 146.

1.4 The Development of Religion

Having ascertained the true origin of totemism, Freud was faced with the equally difficult issue of how such early forms developed into the more familiar, sophisticated, contemporary institutional religions of his era. We will moment-arily see how Freud, in developing his views on this historical trajectory, once again relied on the anthropological literature of his day. But, before we do, it is equally important to note the influence of another figure: his heir turned apostate, Carl Jung.

In the preface to *Totem and Taboo* Freud confesses that, among other things, it was Jung's emerging notion of a "collective unconscious" populated by archetypes that provided the "first stimulus" for his book. Indeed, he goes on to say that he aims to provide a "methodological contrast" to Jung.[15] Given that Freud and Jung were slowly in the process of an intellectual divorce, it is notable that Freud thought enough of Jung's emerging theory to offer a psychoanalytic version of it. Indeed, Freud countered Jung with his own theory of version of the "collective mind" dominated by one (and only one) "universal archetype," namely Oedipus. It is Freud's version of the collective mind that becomes his solution to the problem of social psychology and the historical driver of new cultural forms and expressions.

What, then, was Freud's psychoanalytic version of the collective mind? In formulating this concept Freud turned to biology and the phylogenetic trans-mission of species memories, events and traumas. Freud became convinced that the human species as a whole shares certain historical traumas (notably the primal deed). There is, then, what he called an "archaic heritage" that "com-prises not only dispositions but also subject-matter – memory-traces of the experience of earlier generations."[16] In order to make this work, he had to argue for what he called "the inheritance of psychical dispositions."[17] This has been taken as a reference to the theories of the biologist Jean-Baptiste Lamarck (1744–1829), who had earlier posited the inheritance of acquired characteristics (the modern-day theoretical version being that of transgenerational epigenet-ics). Freud goes on to say that if one accepts such an argument, then "we have bridged the gulf between individual and group psychology: we can deal with people as we do with an individual neurotic."[18] Interestingly enough, this forces Freud to amend his concept of the unconscious, particularly as it relates to individual belief. In *Totem and Taboo* (later elaborated in his *The Future of an Illusion*) Freud notes that psychoanalysis teaches us a singular point:

---

[15] Ibid., pp. xiii–xiv.   [16] Freud, *Moses and Monotheism*, S. E., vol. 23, p. 99.
[17] Freud, *Totem and Taboo*, S. E., vol. 13, p. 158.
[18] Freud, *Moses and Monotheism*, S. E., vol. 23, p. 100.

the conception of God found in any individual is "formed in the likeness of his father, that his personal relation to God depends on his relation to his father in the flesh and oscillates and changes along with that relation, and that at bottom God is nothing other than an exalted father."[19] But, having adopted the theory of phylogenesis, this means that the individual's image of God is both phylogenetically and ontogenetically determined. Freud later (1923) confirmed this when, in speaking of a religious believer, he noted that "the ideational image belonging to his childhood is preserved and becomes merged with the inherited memory-traces of the primal father to form the individual's idea of God."[20]

What does this mean for the historical trajectory of collective religion? We know that for Freud the primal deed was the beginning of society, morality and religion. Additionally, if all humans (in the phylogenetic dimension of their unconscious) suffer from the dim guilt of the primal deed (i.e., Freud's version of original sin), then that trauma continues to exert pressure on history, social institutions, morality and religion, much like a collective "return of the repressed." So it is that Freud states that all historical developments in religion exist in relation to the primal deed: they "are reactions to the same great event with which civilization began" and "attempts at solving the same problem" (which is to say, the shared guilt and psychic upheaval initiated by the primal deed).[21] The strength and power (as well as the promise of protection and guidance) of the primal father, collectively forgotten, buried and repressed, seeks a "return." Through the course of history, then, Freud saw a natural gradient toward monotheism and patriarchy, not necessarily because they are more rational or better structures but because human collectives are unconsciously determined to follow the dynamic designs of the inherited, collective, "phylogenetic unconscious." Adding further sophistication to this, and buying into a thesis widely shared by the early anthropologists who posited a socio-evolutionary thrust to human history, civilization and the development of religions, he proposed the progression of religion from a pre-religious phase (animism, totemism) to an institutional phase (religion proper) to a post-religious phase (science). There was a correlation between "the development of men's view of the universe and the stages of an individual's libidinal development."[22] In this progression

> [t]he animistic phase would correspond to narcissism both chronologically and in content; the religious phase would correspond to the stage of object-choice of which the characteristic is the child's attachment to his parents; while the scientific phase would have an exact counterpart in the stage at

---

[19] Freud, *Totem and Taboo*, S. E., vol. 13, p. 147.
[20] Freud, "A Seventeenth-Century Demonological Neurosis," S. E., vol. 19, p. 85.
[21] Freud, *Totem and Taboo*, S. E., vol. 13, p. 145.   [22] Ibid., p. 90.

which an individual has reached maturity, has renounced the pleasure principle [and] adjusted himself to reality.[23]

As we will detail more in the sections to come, one can already see in such
formulations Freud's desire to frame psychoanalysis as the logical heir to what
he thought to be a declining monotheism.

1.5 The Advent of True Monotheism

Freud remained somewhat sweeping with regard to details about the precise
development from totemism to institutional religion and beyond. He lays out
a general dynamic sequence: primal deed, remorse/guilt, the creation of totemism
as a form of the return of the repressed, the eventual morphing of a "father-animal"
to an idealized "father-God" (the totem being "the first form of father-surrogate"
and the idea of God "a later one"),[24] but he glosses over the development of the
"concept" of God as coming "from some unknown source."[25] With respect to
individual religious traditions, he says little about the emergence of matriarchal
social structures and the tradition of mother goddesses, only noting that they likely
preceded patriarchies and male-gendered monotheisms. However, being but inad-
equate and partial returns of the repressed, they were destined to eventually give
way to them (which is to say that the father is more powerful than the mother).[26]
Unfortunately his treatment of Western monotheisms (Judaism, Christianity,
Islam) is equally dubious and only somewhat more detailed.

Freud's view on the advent of the first "true" monotheism is carried forward
in his last book on religion, *Moses and Monotheism* (1939). His argument has
essentially four steps. The first is that Moses was culturally and biologically an
Egyptian. Of course this differs from the biblical narrative of Moses in Exodus,
which portrays him as a Jew born of the tribe of Levi who, when the pharaoh
ordered all male Jewish children drowned, was fortunate enough to have his
mother send him down the river in a small basket, there to be picked up and
raised by the pharaoh's daughter. Freud counters this by accepting the historical
scholarship of J. H. Breasted and Eduard Meyer, who argued that the name
Moses is of Egyptian origin. Mixing in psychoanalytic interpretations of "hero
myths," Freud concludes that it is probable that "Moses was an Egyptian . . .
whom the legend was designed to turn into a Jew."[27] He goes on to suggest that
Moses was a nobleman, perhaps the governor of a border province where he
came into contact with Semitic tribes.[28]

---

[23] Ibid.   [24] Ibid., p. 148.

[25] Ibid., p. 147 (see also Freud, *Moses and Monotheism*, S. E., vol. 23, p. 133).

[26] Ibid., pp. 144, 149.   [27] Freud, *Moses and Monotheism*, S. E., vol. 23, p. 15.

[28] Ibid., pp. 60–61.

The second is that Moses created the Jews and gave them monotheism ("[I]t was this one man Moses who created the Jews"[29]). Drawing on the historical studies of his day Freud observes that well before Moses Egyptian culture valorized polytheism, replete with narratives about death and the afterlife (as evinced in the narratives around the god Osiris). The change from polytheism to monotheism was implemented by Pharaoh Amenhotep IV (who later changed his name to Ikhnaton), who expunged all traces of Egyptian polytheism in favor of a strict monotheism based on the sun god Aton. Significantly, this was the world's first monotheism: exclusive (there is only one God) and immaterial (prohibiting all images), marginalizing magical and mythical elements, disdaining ceremonials and sacrifices, enforcing circumcision and valorizing the more abstract ideals of ethics, justice and truth. It was this religion, argues Freud, that the Egyptian nobleman Moses was socialized into and accepted as his own. When Amenhotep/Ikhnaton died and subsequent social shifts undermined the Aton monotheism, Moses left Egypt, taking with him the Jewish inhabitants of his province. As their leader, he avowed that they were his "chosen people," bequeathing them monotheism.[30]

Having presented his preferred historical narrative, Freud then turns to psychoanalysis. Why did the Jews accept Moses and monotheism? Part of the reason may be simply developmental, namely Moses was a father figure and protector. However, given that this was the first appearance of "true" monotheism, Freud argued that a deeper, phylogenetic explanation was needed. Recall that Freud, in *Totem and Taboo*, had suggested that the return of the (phylogenetic) repressed would eventually lead to patriarchy and a true monotheism (by which he meant the return of the primal father). Moses and the one and only God "behind him," then, were nothing less than the external event that awakened the dynamic power of the phylogenetic unconscious. As Freud put it, what Moses brought was not so much a novelty as it was "the revival of an experience in the primeval ages of the human family which had long ago vanished from men's conscious memory."[31] With Moses the memory of the primal father came alive:

> The first effect of meeting the being who had so long been missed and longed for was overwhelming and was like the traditional description of the law-giving from Mount Sinai. Admiration, awe and thankfulness for having found grace in his eyes – the religion of Moses knew none but these positive feelings towards the father-god. The conviction of his irresistibility, the submission to

---

[29] Ibid., p. 106.

[30] The scholarship Freud cites is J. H. Breasted, *A History of Egypt* (London: Charles Scribner's Sons, 1906) and *The Dawn of Conscience* (London: Charles Scribner's Sons, 1934); A. Weigall, *The Life and Times of Ikhnaton* (London: Thornton Butterworth, 1910); A. Erman, *Die Ägyptische Religion* (Berlin: G. Reimer, 1905).

[31] Freud, *Moses and Monotheism*, S. E., vol. 23, p. 129.

his will, could not have been more unquestioning in the helpless and intimi-
dated son of the father of the horde . . . a rapture of devotion to God was thus
the first reaction to the return of the great father.[32]

Freud adds that such intense awe and admiration, being feelings beyond the normal
range of the personal unconscious, required a correspondingly altered state: "only
religious ecstasy can bring them back."[33] In other words, what is uncovered in that
altered state known as religious ecstasy is the contents of not only the personal
unconscious but more, that of the universal memory-traces that define the content
of our phylogenetically transmitted archaic heritage. To be sure, while this begins
to sound like the religious overtones evident in Jung's view of archetypes, it should
be noted that we are dealing not with some spiritual essence but the dynamic return
of the phylogenic repressed, the content of which is comprised of memories and
traumas of actual historical events. The powerful figure of Moses was but the
instigator of the return of those memories of the fearsome and majestic primal
father that were repressed in the phylogenic unconscious.

Importantly, there were some notable differences between the primal father and
his totemism and the monotheism of Moses. Freud deemed the latter a cultural
advance in that the Mosaic prohibition on images was linked to the renunciation
of id-based instinctual desire, ethical maturity and intellectuality (i.e., the rise of
the ego and reality testing). The prohibition of images tended to favor memories,
reflections and deductions over the inevitable illusions of sense perception and the
influence of developmental determinants. This "progress in spirituality" (as Freud
calls it), mediated through subsequent generations, was a stepping stone to the
next cultural advance: the rise of science. In essence, then, Freud inserted Moses
and the prohibition against images as part of the evolutionary view of culture he
had held since *Totem and Taboo*. Psychoanalysis, as a form of science, would be
framed by Freud as the logical cultural heir to what he thought to be a declining
monotheism.

Freud's narrative did not stop there. The next step in the historical process is
that the Jews murdered Moses in a reenactment of the primal deed. Here Freud
drew upon the scholarship of the historian and biblical scholar Ernst Sellin who,
starting in 1922, claimed that his reading of the book of Hosea suggested that
Moses had been murdered. While this thesis was for many quite dubious, it fit
perfectly with Freud's stress on the power of the return of the phylogenetic
repressed.[34] We have already seen that Moses awakened the grandeur of the
primal father (the acceptance of Moses was the "re-establishment of the primal

---

[32] Ibid., pp. 133–134.   [33] Ibid., p. 134.

[34] Y. H. Yerushalmi provides a critical look at Sellin and Freud's appropriation of his thought in
chapter 2 of his *Freud's Moses: Judaism Terminable and Interminable* (New Haven, CT: Yale
University Press, 1991).

father in his historic rights"[35]) and that the monotheistic prohibition against images and stress on justice and truth were advances. But the strength of the phylogenetic unconscious overwhelmed reason and morality, and a historical moment of phylogenetically driven "acting out" against the "father" (Moses and behind him the primal father) occurred. Predictably, the return of the (phylogenetic) repressed led to the repetition of the primal deed. Freud thought that he had corroborated Sellin's thesis by bringing in psychoanalytically framed phylogenetic factors.

Finally, Freud posits that after the murder of Moses the Jews abandoned monotheism. Once again following the researches of Eduard Meyer, Freud narrates a history that has the Jews wandering in the wilderness for generations, engaging other wandering Jewish tribes (the Midianites in particular), eventually idealizing yet another Moses (the "Midianite Moses") who introduced them to a new god: Yahweh (the volcano God), described by Freud as "uncanny" and "bloodthirsty."[36] In other words, departing from the normative understanding of the biblical narrative, Freud posits that there were two Moses and two religions. However, as time passed several factors served to bring the Jews back to the Egyptian Moses and his monotheism: an oral tradition that kept the memory of the latter alive, the prophetic tradition and, most importantly, the increase in guilt and longing fueled by the buried memory of the murder of Moses (and behind him the primal father). Freud defends his acceptance of this revisionist narrative by claiming that the biblical narrative had been "distorted by the influence of powerful tendentious purposes and embellished by the products of poetic invention."[37]

1.6 Christianity and Islam after Moses

Freud's view that the Jews murdered Moses (which amounts to the "acting out" of the "return of the phylogenetic repressed") set up his view of Christianity and Islam. In the case of Islam (which Freud referred to as the "Mahommedan religion"), Freud thought it to be what he called an "abbreviated repetition" of Judaism. He goes on to suggest that Muhammed originally intended to accept Judaism "in full for himself and his people" but that its development was stunted in that Muhammed never suffered the fate of Moses.[38] Beyond that, one searches in vain for any more of Freud's commentary on Islam.

---

[35] Freud, *Moses and Monotheism*, S. E., vol. 23, p. 86.   [36] Ibid., p. 34.   [37] Ibid., p. 41.

[38] Ibid., p. 92. Freud said little about Islam, but there is a growing psychoanalytic literature concerning it. See, for example, O. El Shakry, *The Arabic Freud* (Princeton, NJ: Princeton University Press, 2017); S. Aktar (ed.), *The Crescent and the Couch* (New York: Jason Aronson, 2008); J. Jones, *Blood That Cries Out from the Earth* (New York: Oxford University Press, 2008); E. Said, *Freud and the Non-European* (New York: Verso, 2003); F. Benslama, *Psychoanalysis and the Challenge of Islam* (Minneapolis: University of Minnesota Press, 2009).

As for Christianity, Freud thought that Judaism had set the stage in that the murder of Moses created the expectation that a "Messiah" would return. Freud goes on to say that for Christians the expectation of a Messiah became projected onto the figure of Jesus. St. Paul carried the ball farther by formulating a "son" religion. The latter had the advantage of admitting to the "original sin" within us all in that Jesus, as son, represents the "band of brothers" while his sacrifice (crucifixion) is the redemptive act that atoned for our collective guilt. Indeed, the popularity of Christianity lies precisely in that we all understand the primal crime in some deep way and so seek collective atonement. Moreover, if original sin is bound up with the primal murder and the crucifixion understood to be atonement for collective guilt, then the ritual of communion becomes a later transformation of the totem meal (one "eats" the flesh and blood of God). Freud then interjects an interesting twist: while Christ "saved" the band of brothers from the guilt of original sin (primal parricide), so too did he accomplish the "other" side of ambivalence, the wish to entirely displace the father: a father-religion was replaced by a son-religion. Freud, then, drew a direct connection between the primal deed, the creation of totemism, the murder of Moses, the expectation of the Messiah and the birth of a "son religion." While the murder of the son was an advance in that people intuitively knew that a member of the "brother band" had to be sacrificed, there was also, relative to Judaism, some regression that accompanied Christianity: the affirmation of magical, mystical and superstitious elements; the valorization of ceremonials and rituals; and a retarding of intellectuality and freedom of thought.[39]

1.7 Contemporary Religion: Freud's Definitional Strategy

We have already seen how Durkheim and James entered into what can be called the "definitional debate" concerning religion. In building on that commentary in the previous section, we can note that so too did Jung who, by way of seizing on the mystical element within religion, offered that "by the term 'religion' I do not mean a creed," adding that creeds, and indeed all forms of religious doctrine, are but "codified and dogmatized forms of original religious experience."[40] In fact, Jung's view of what constituted "original religious experience" was dependent on Rudolph Otto, a noted theologian and comparative scholar of religion of his era, who framed such matters in terms of the experience of the "numinosum." By the latter Otto meant a direct, mystical encounter with the divine described as mysterious,

---

[39] Ibid., pp. 86ff.
[40] C. Jung, *Psychology and Religion* (New Haven, CT: Yale University Press, 1977 [1938]), pp. 4–6.

nonrational, "wholly Other," awesome, frightening, and fascinating ("mysterium tremendum et fascinans").[41] This fit Jung's own psychological model of religion well, for experiences of "tremendum et fascinans" were precisely those which characterized the encounter with the collective unconscious and its archetypes. In this he was closer to James than Durkheim, which one would expect in that both James and Jung were advocates of a psycho-spirituality.

Given this, as we have already indicated, one would expect Freud to enter into the definitional debate. To start, it is the case that in his two most noted works on religion (*The Future of an Illusion* [1927]; *Civilization and Its Discontents* [1930]), Freud said that he was concerned not so much with the origins and development of religion (as in *Totem and Taboo*) but with "the finished body of religious ideas as it is transmitted by civilization to the individual," further clarifying the latter as consisting of "present-day white Christian" institutional religion.[42] Freud then went further to qualify the latter, saying that it pertained to the understanding of religion found in what he called the "common-man's" religion:

> In my *Future of an Illusion* I was concerned ... with what the common man understands by his religion – with the system of doctrines and promises which on the one hand explains to him the riddles of this world with enviable completeness, and, on the other, assures him that a careful Providence will watch over his life and will compensate him in a future existence for any frustration he suffers here. The common man cannot imagine this Providence otherwise than in the figure of an enormously exalted father. Only such a being can understand the needs of the children of men and be softened by their prayers and placated by the signs of their remorse.[43]

To be sure, Freud was aware of more sophisticated philosophical and theological attempts to transcend this more infantile religion of the common-man. The problem with the latter is that they replaced what he called the "mighty personality of religious doctrines" with "an impersonal, shadowy and abstract principle."[44] Abstract renderings of the divine did not offer a "higher, purer concept of God" so much as an "insubstantial shadow" of the exalted Father God. For Freud, then, such attempts stretched "the meaning of words until they retain scarcely anything of their original sense."[45] So it is that, in entering the definitional debates on the "what" of religion, Freud makes clear that his strategy had isolated the only deserving definition of religion ("the only religion

---

[41] Ibid.   [42] Freud, *Future of an Illusion*, S. E., vol. 21, pp. 24, 20.

[43] Freud, *Civilization and Its Discontents*, S. E., vol. 22, p. 74; *Future of an Illusion*, S. E., vol. 21, pp. 30–31.

[44] Freud, *Future of an Illusion*, S. E., vol. 21, p. 32.   [45] Ibid.

which ought to bear that name").[46] This is a crucial fact for the scholar of religion, given that the debate on the meaning and use of the term "religion" has animated the halls of the academic study of religion for decades. What becomes clear through tracing the history of such debates is that, to a large extent, perhaps even a determinative one, scholars of religion have done more to "invent" the term than anyone else.[47] In the case of Freud, his definitional strategy was focused on the common-man and assumed institutionalized patriarchal forms of sociocultural power whose normative expression was centered in the monotheistic "mighty personality" of an exalted Father-God.[48]

1.8 Freud's Interpretation of Religion: The Classic-Reductive Approach

The matter, then, turns to how he interpreted its psychoanalytic meaning. The general scholarly consensus is that Freud championed what can be called the "classic-reductive" analysis of religion. Put briefly, Freud thought that religion was a form of illusion that catered to a person's sense of helplessness, the existential need for protection, care, guidance and justice. Religious ideas "are illusions, fulfillments of the oldest, strongest and most urgent wishes of mankind."[49] As Freud went on to specify:

> The terrifying impression of helplessness in childhood aroused the need for protection – for protection through love – which was provided by the father; and the recognition that this helplessness lasts throughout life made it necessary to cling to the existence of the father, but this time a more powerful one. Thus the benevolent ruler of a divine Providence allays our fear of the dangers of life; the establishment of a moral world-order ensures the fulfillment of the demands of justice, which have so often remained unfulfilled in human civilization; and the prolongation of earthly existence in a future life provides the local and temporal framework in which these wish-fulfilments shall take place. Answers to the riddles that tempt the curiosity of man, such as how the universe began or what the relation is between body and mind, are developed in conformity with the underlying assumptions of this system. It is

---

[46] Freud, *Civilization and Its Discontents*, S. E., vol. 21, p. 74.

[47] Debates concerning the definitional problem are as old as the field itself. See W. C. Smith, *The Meaning and End of Religion* (Minneapolis, MN: Fortress Press, 1991[1962]); J. Z. Smith, *Imagining Religion* (Chicago, IL: University of Chicago Press, 1988); Russell T. McCutcheon, *Studying Religion* (New York: Routledge, 2018); J. J. Thatamanil, *Circling the Elephant: A Comparative Theory of Religious Diversity* (New York: Fordham University Press, 2020). The failure to acknowledge and comprehend the implications of Freud's narrow definitional strategy is, alongside conceptual misreadings and an absence of critical reading skills, at the root of the intransigence of Freud's defenders (e.g. M. Hewitt, 2022).

[48] Much has been written about the role of anti-Semitism, the Habsburg regime and Catholicism in impacting Freud's understanding of and response to religion. See, for example, W. B. Parsons, *Freud and Religion: Advancing the Dialogue* (especially chapter 1) and P. Cooper-White, *Old and Dirty Gods: Religion, Antisemitism, and the Origins of Psychoanalysis* (New York: Routledge, 2018).

[49] Freud, *Future of an Illusion*, S. E., vol. 21, p. 30.

also an enormous relief to the individual psyche if the conflicts of its childhood arising from the father-complex – conflicts which it has never wholly overcome – are removed from it and brought to a solution which is universally accepted.[50]

Freud did not equate his use of the term "illusion" solely with respect to outright error and falsehood. In qualifying his use of the term, Freud notes that it is possible that God exists and that a Messiah will come and found a golden age. However, the high degree of improbability of such things leads him to wonder less about their possible truth and more about the motivation of those who believe in what he thinks is absolute nonsense. Turning psychoanalytic (and here one hears echoes of his works on dreams), his answer is that they believe due to the power of certain wishes: for protection from both natural and human forces, for consolation and justice and for simple answers to the "big" questions of life. Becoming even more psychoanalytic, he suggests that such motivations follow a psychological gradient born of childhood helplessness when one's anxieties were assuaged by the presence of the earthly father. In facing the exigencies of life one responds by regressing back to a childish form of adaptation linked to the relation one had to one's father.

Freud thought that there was a better alternative than that of "regressive adaptation." In *Future of an Illusion* he stated his own preference with respect to what the Dutch writer Multatuli framed as the "twin" Gods of Logos (Reason) and Ananke (Necessity) – "Gods" that valorized the empirical findings of science and a psychoanalytically informed, mature adaptation to reality. Such mature individuals lived without the crutch of religious illusions, were capable of successfully adapting to the demands of civilization through sublimation, had a healthy superego and lacked debilitating forms of neuroses. Relative to that standard, the common-man, in choosing the cultural option of religious belief, abandons reason and performs an act ("regressive adaptation") which amounts to rehearsing the childish solution to the universal problem of adaptation. This move allows for threats to one's sense of self-esteem and identity to be solved by a means (e.g., prayer) through which one's anxieties are assuaged. Unfulfilled desires and perceived injustices stemming from fate, civilization and other people are dealt with through a prescription (the confession of faith) that will eventuate in one's ascension to heaven while one's enemies descend to eternal suffering. Again, the answers to what Freud referred to as the "riddles of the universe" are found in a long history of religious intellectuals who, basing their thought on revealed scripture and tradition, provide authoritative dictums. With regard to the latter, Freud suggests that certain religious ideas are so

---

[50] Ibid.

improbable that they move from "illusions" to "delusions." As he put it, when the degree of unlikeliness of religious ideas are such that they are "so incompatible with everything we have laboriously discovered about the reality of the world," then it is best to "compare them ... to delusions."[51]

1.9 Religion and Therapy

Despite the preceeding, Freud lent a qualified, tentative approval to the positive, adaptive function of religious forms of therapy. In an earlier paper titled "On Psychotherapy" (1905) he notes that in a general sense psychotherapy, of which psychoanalysis is but one specified form, "is in no way a modern method of treatment" but "the most ancient form of therapy in medicine," going on to say that "there are many ways and means of practicing psychotherapy. All that lead to recovery are good."[52] In distinguishing psychoanalysis from other forms of therapy, Freud relies on Leonardo da Vinci's distinction between *per via di porre* (the application of a substance onto a canvas, as exemplified in painting) and *per via di levare* (the uncovering and chipping away at a surface to reveal the art within, as with sculpture). Freud allied religious therapies with "suggestive-supportive" types of therapy and psychoanalysis with analytic, uncovering techniques. Religious forms of therapy, being suggestive-supportive in nature, operated by monitoring and containing the unconscious in an "experience-distant" fashion through public symbols and narratives. In the event of mental distress, religious therapies functioned by manipulating unconscious content through the empathic mediation of idealized religious functionaries (e.g., priests), various forms of inner work (e.g., prayer, contemplation) and the reintegration of the neurotic into a supportive community and its regnant worldview.

As evinced in his correspondence with the lay analyst and minister Oskar Pfister, one finds Freud noting that the two types of therapy (suggestive-supportive and analytic) could be combined; psychoanalysis was an "impartial tool which both priest and layman can use in the service of the sufferer" and that psychoanalysis could be "extraordinarily helpful" in "pastoral work."[53] It is also indicated in some of his case histories, famously exemplified in that concerning the "wolf man." There Freud observes how religious narratives and symbols helped him by putting "a restraint on his sexual impulses by affording them a sublimation and a safe mooring; it lowered the importance of

---

[51] Ibid., p. 31.

[52] Freud, "On Psychotherapy," S. E., vol. 7, pp. 257–270. See also S. Kakar, *Shamans, Mystics, Doctors* (New York: Alfred A. Knopf, 1982).

[53] H. Meng and E. L. Freud (eds.), *Psychoanalysis and Faith: The Letters of Sigmund Freud and Oskar Pfister* (New York: Basic Books, 1963), p. 17.

his family relationships and, thus, protected him from the threat of isolation by giving him access to the great community of mankind."[54] As a result, "the untamed and fear-ridden child became social, well-behaved, and amenable to education."[55] Again, in his less-acknowledged analysis of the "demonological possession" (the religious way of thinking about neuroses) of the seventeeth-century painter Christoph Haizmann, Freud showed how the latter's neurotic melancholy, based in his ambivalent relation to his father, was nonetheless therapeutically "worked through" by means of the accoutrements of the church. The latter included therapeutic intervention by idealized, empathic church functionaries (priests) who elicited and addressed Haizmann's conflicts through a deft, ritualistic use of the "cultural containers" of God (the "good" father) and Satan (the "bad" father). It also included offering Haizmann an eventual home in a holy order, which, by enjoining him to live a life of asceticism, resulted in a stay of his melancholy.[56] Even so, Freud found religious forms of therapy problematic – a fact we will explore later in this Element.

1.10 Religion and Society

Freud is often read, quite rightly, as analyzing the role of religious faith in the life of the individual believer. But many of his books on religion also challenged existing religious institutions, dogma and social structures. In other words, "applied" psychoanalysis was an effort to occasion social structural change as well as to enjoin one to personal transformation.

Part of Freud's motivation in doing so stemmed from his own biography and experiences with religious racism. The biographers of Freud have noted that in his adolescence, and with the blessings of his family, Freud initially had designs on a political career. In fact, he was deeply involved in student political organizations during his stay at the University of Vienna. His aspirations came to an end when the sociopolitical atmosphere in Vienna was dominated by anti-Semitic forces in the 1880s. His dream life (particularly his dream of his uncle with the "yellow beard") as well as his letters to his fiancée, Martha Bernays, indicate that rising anti-Semitism impacted his choice of career. His turn to psychoanalysis, then, had another function. If he could not change the political culture he could seek another means to change it by offering a praxis (the psychological clinic) that could reform the personality: transformed people transform culture. A political career was a nonstarter but psychoanalysis could

---

[54] Freud, "From the History of an Infantile Neurosis," S. E., vol. 17, pp. 114–115.   [55] Ibid.

[56] Freud, "A Neurosis of Demonological Possession in the Seventeenth Century," S. E., vol. 19, pp. 69–105. Freud's more cursory analysis was given greater psychoanalytic sophistication in E. Erikson's analysis of Luther in his *Young Man Luther* (New York: W. W. Norton, 1958). For more cases of the suggestive-supportive type, see S. Kakar, *Shamans, Mystics, Doctors*.

be a means to conquer malignant social forces and institutions (like religion) that impeded social justice while providing a basis for establishing a new social whole. As one commentator put it: "Freud, the most political of adolescents, turned in the wake of his political disillusionment to the philosophical, scientific realm to express his radical impulses."[57]

The idea that applied psychoanalysis could occasion social-structural change is evident in his 1930 work *Civilization and Its Discontents* (the German title being *Das Unbehagen in der Kultur*). Humans are dissatisfied and uneasy in civilization because our innate aggressive instinct makes us asocial and unwilling to renounce wishes. Freud adds a corollary to this: our dissatisfaction is increased by what he called the "unpsychological" proceedings of society, particularly its commands and institutions, of which religion stands at the forefront. How religion exacerbates *unbehagen* in people can best be seen in its function as the "cultural superego." The very first cultural superego was the totem, which functioned (as do all cultural superegos) to inhibit the natural antisocial, aggressive instincts in people through idealization of the totem (which must not be killed) and taboos (early moral laws). Eventually the latter morphed into traditional forms of monotheism. While the content of the two differed, the psychological fact remains that through idealizing and internalizing the commands of the religious (cultural) superego one's own self-perception and relation to others and reality are formed. Freud endeavored to provide what can be called the "developmental infrastructure" to even the highest commands, ideals and doctrines promoted by the religio-cultural superego. Any doctrine or command that does not take this infrastructure into account invariably runs the risk of creating heightened guilt and unease.

The import of this becomes clear in Freud's rejoinder to Immanuel Kant and his grand ethical law (i.e., the "categorial imperative"). Freud noted that while it is noble to think that Kant's moral law "couples the conscience within with the starry Heavens" and that a "pious man might well be tempted to honour these two things as the masterpieces of creation," that in actual fact many have little or even no conscience or sense of justice.[58] As Freud put it: "God has done an uneven and careless piece of work."[59] What he meant is that such ethical laws all too often neglect the developmental origins and determinants of the superego (i.e., one's "conscience"), and how a faulty superego affects, even perverts, the noble implementation of ethical principles and legal rulings. While the potential mendacity of religious commands had been indelibly imprinted on him as a Jew at the University of Vienna, it was reinforced during the Great War. In his little

---

[57] See J. McGrath, *Freud's Discovery of Psychoanalysis: The Politics of Hysteria* (Ithaca, NY: Cornell University Press, 1986), p. 109.
[58] Freud, *New Introductory Lectures on Psychoanalysis*, S. E., vol. 22, p. 61.   [59] Ibid.

paper "The Disillusionment of War" (1915) he observed the general disillusion-ment that occurred for many when they realized how even the most cultured individuals and those in power seemed incapable of acting in a civilized manner. They were, in Freud's terms, "cultural hypocrites," by which he meant those who, seemingly abiding by noble commands, actually used the latter in the service of untransformed, selfish and base instinctual drives. Mendacity, lying, sheer barbarism, unbridled lust for power and censorship ruled the day. In other words, in Freud's hands both religion and politics could be understood as but an "epiphenomenal manifestation of psychic forces."[60] Certainly Freud would see in the contemporary merging between religion and politics evidence of the same. As a counter, applied psychoanalysis provides the kind of moral educa-tion and social structural change needed to expose and reform the developmen-tally challenged.[61]

The classic example linked to this point is Freud's analysis of the Christian love command. Initially one might take it to be in the service of Eros, being one of the mental assets of civilization designed to counter aggressive, antisocial instincts toward civilization and the "other" in all of its forms. However, in its unqualified, extreme form, which insists that one love universally, Freud thought it unpsychological and impossible to fulfill, for it is based on the assumption that our ego has unlimited mastery over the id. If more is demanded (in this case, to love universally) than one is capable of producing, then there will be psychological consequences. As Freud put it, "revolt will be produced in him or a neurosis, or he will be made unhappy."[62] He went on to attribute the origin of this extreme framing of the love command to developmental factors, specifically that issuing from the preoedipal phase. The command to love universally compels because it caters to the nostalgic pull of, in fact is the developmental residue of, a time when love was abundant and one did not distinguish between objects (namely, the preoedipal developmental phase of union with the mother). One is enjoined to love everyone as oneself because it recalls an ideal time when in fact that was the case.

This analysis shows how a command, which in reality is ruled at least in part by a developmental infrastructure, is taken up by the cultural superego and reified, thus idealized as issuing from an unchanging divine reality. It is then internalized, there to create guilt and *unbehagen*. The solution is to shear such commands of their developmental pull and, by subjecting them to rational discourse, offer a better, revised version that can be implemented in a psychologically responsible way. Freud himself did just this by arguing for

[60] C. Schorske, *Fin-de-Siècle Vienna* (New York: Vintage, 1981), p. 183.

[61] Freud, "The Disillusionment of the War," S. E., vol. 14, pp. 275–289.

[62] Freud, *Civilization and Its Discontents*, S. E., vol. 21, p. 143.

a qualified view of the love command. He noted that one might love the other if they represent high ideals that are worthy, or friends and relatives of one's own friends and relatives. He railed against loving a stranger who might be not only hostile to one but also wishes one emotional or physical harm. That would be a disservice to those one does in fact love, for it would fail to distinguish the moral worth of people and perhaps authorize, if not justify, the asocial behavior of the "enemies" of civilization. Wallwork has argued that this stance is close to a Jewish form of other-regard based on the principles of respect and fair reciprocity, the latter informed by the knowledge of the innate aggressiveness of humans and the idea that most cannot overcome this or even become aware of it.[63] So it is that Freud is willing to say that if the stranger embodies one's ideals then, yes, one can love him; that if the neighbor "behaves differently, if he shows me consideration and foreberance as a stranger, I am ready to treat him in the same way."[64] Again, reciprocity is indicated when Freud says the following: "If this grandiose commandment had run 'Love thy neighbor as they neighbor loves thee,' I should not take exception to it."[65] Even more problematic is the fact that an unqualified version of the love command could have serious cultural consequences, as is evident in his linkage of the love command to what he called the "narcissism of minor differences." To that we will attend in the last section of this Element.

1.11 Psychoanalysis As the Secular Cure of Souls

While deeply critical of the cultural superego, Freud was also careful to speak of its more positive dimension. Given the human propensity to aggression, civilization needed a cultural superego to defend itself and the "group." Religion had served the aims of Eros, of creating unity. So it is that he states that religion "has clearly performed great services for human civilization. It has contributed much towards the taming of the asocial instincts ... It has ruled human society for many thousands of years and has time to show what it can achieve."[66] Despite fostering guilt and the general "unpsychological proceedings" of religious institutions, the value of religion for civilization lay in its cultural function: those rules, commands and regulations designed to offset man's natural aggressive, antisocial tendencies. Freud then added an important qualification, however. He thought we were at a "turning point" in history when religion was no longer capable of being functional for either individuals or civilization. "It is to be supposed that a turning-away from religion is bound to occur with the fatal

---

[63] E. Wallwork, *Psychoanalysis and Ethics* (New Haven, CT: Yale University Press, 1991).

[64] Freud, *Civilization and Its Discontents*, S. E., vol. 21, p. 110.   [65] Ibid.

[66] Freud, *Future of an Illusion*, S. E., vol. 21, p. 37.

inevitability of a process of growth, and that we find ourselves at this very juncture in the middle of that phase of development."[67] In other words, in once again entering into sizable debates within the academic study of religion, Freud thought that secularization was an undisputed fact. His reason for thinking so was notably thin: the rise of science would invariably occasion the disillusionment with religious tenets and worldviews. While admitting that the latter is "perhaps not the only reason," he stresses how "criticism" and "the scientific spirit" have "whittled away the evidential value of religious documents" while "natural science has shown up the errors in them."[68] He was convinced that, in this process of growth, "there is no stopping."[69]

For Freud this amounted to nothing less than a coming cultural catastrophe. To offset the danger to civilization, Freud offered a twofold agenda. First, with regards to individuals, he sought means to educate and sublimate the instincts, strengthen the ego, shore up the superego, and make as many people as possible vehicles of civilization. Linked to the latter were Freud's suggestions concerning changes at the social-structural level. Specifically, he sought to create new institutions that would replace religion in a manner commensurate with the aim of keeping civilization whole while fulfilling the psychological needs of the human populace.

With regard to individuals, Freud was convinced that subsequent generations, imbued with the spirit of scientific inquiry and reason, would be more willing to accept rational reasons for following the precepts and renunciations of civilization as opposed to the fear- and guilt-driven myths of religion.[70] New generations will "be ready for its sake to make the sacrifices as regards work and instinctual satisfaction" and will "be able to do without coercion."[71] This rendering of the power of reason led Freud to be "optimistic about the future of mankind."[72] This would be aided by other changes in the educational curriculum. Freud advocated for the deconstruction of any religiously driven educational system in that he thought it not only heightened repression and neurosis but also inhibited the mature development of a curious, inquiring and critical intellect. In particular, he cautioned against premature religious influence, which meant that all too often children were socialized into a religious worldview well before they were interested in or even capable of considering their existential relevance and intellectual worth. The net effect was that later, when the child's intellect awakened, religious tenets were, as a result of emotional bonds, unconscious forces and cultural norms, that much harder to challenge.[73]

---

[67] Ibid., p. 43. [68] Ibid., p. 38. [69] Ibid. [70] Ibid., p. 8. [71] Ibid. [72] Ibid., p. 53.
[73] Ibid., p. 49.

Perhaps the most notable structural change Freud advocated was the insertion of psychoanalysis as a means to educate and sublimate the instincts, thus not only replacing the function religion once had but also doing it one better in that it could help people to realistically and humanely adapt to the exigencies of life. This aim, implicit throughout *The Future of an Illusion*, became explicit in Freud's letters to the Protestant pastor Oskar Pfister. There Freud revealed the "secret link" between *The Future of an Illusion* and an earlier book he wrote on the importance of lay analysts. The latter was written to protect psychoanalysis from being governed solely by the medical profession while *The Future of an Illusion* was written to protect psychoanalysis from the church. So it is that Freud stated to Pfister: "I should like to hand it over to a profession of *lay* curers of souls who ... should not be priests."[74] If civilization had depended on religion to defend against the hostility of the masses, and if religion was on the decline and unable to fulfill its cultural function, then a psychoanalytic secular cure of souls was the needed antidote. What Freud was after, then, was a sea change in the content of the cultural superego: a "triumph of the therapeutic" that valorized psychoanalysis, now understood as a moral science that enjoined one to inwardness, self-knowledge, renunciation, sublimation and increased empathy for the other.

1.12 Freud and Eastern Religions

Finally, most commentators rightly point out Freud reflected mainly on Judaism and Christianity with scant attention to Eastern religions. Part of this is attributable to the fact that in Freud's era relatively little was known of Buddhism and Hinduism. Before 1880, which is to say, when the psychology of religion was but a nascent academic field, the engagement with Eastern religions in Europe and North America was sporadic and piecemeal, informed primarily through the auspices of missionaries, business enterprises, travel and trade. Academic positions in Oriental studies and comparative religion at Ivy League schools and European institutions (including the University of Vienna where Freud studied and taught) were newly minted, giving rise to an initial generation of scholars (e.g., Rudolph Otto, Friedrich Heiler, Max Müller) and the introduction of the first accessible translations (notably the classic *Sacred Books of the East* series in 1875). On the wider cultural scale Eastern religious ideas were only just beginning to be disseminated through the auspices of philosophers and poets (e.g., Nietzsche, Emerson, the Theosophical movement) and visits from Eastern holy men (e.g., Vivekananda, Yogananda), the latter crowned by the World's Parliament of Religion in Chicago (1893).

---

[74] See H. Meng and E.L. Freud, eds., *Psychoanalysis and Faith*, p. 126.

At the same time, this "[O]riental renaissance," as Raymond Schwab once called it, was not wholly lost on those writing in the psychology and religion movement.[75] Freud's written corpus indicates that he was familiar, if but in a cursory way, with many Eastern texts, gods, goddesses and contemporary adepts (e.g., the Upanishads, the Bhagavad Gita and various Buddhist sutras; Kali and Vishnu; Ramakrishna, Vivekananda, Tagore and Gandhi). While Freud's ruminations on Eastern religions can be found scattered throughout his corpus, most scholars point to the first chapter of *Civilization and Its Discontents*, for it is there that Freud refers to Eastern mystical practices and the famous "oceanic feeling."

The man who led Freud down this path was Roman Rolland, a disillusioned Catholic who linked his oceanic feeling to Eastern religions. Rolland cited as evidence of the latter his upcoming biographies of two Hindu saints, Ramakrishna and Vivekananda (which, upon publication, he sent to Freud as a gift). Freud's interpretation of the oceanic feeling was based on Rolland's description in a letter of December 5, 1927. The latter, then, comprises the "case" presented to Freud for interpretation. How did Rolland characterize the oceanic feeling? Many commentators, operating in a post-Jamesian age, think that Rolland's oceanic feeling was but an instance of the familiar episodic "mystical experience" and that Freud interpreted it as a regression to the pre-Oedipal developmental phase he called "primary narcissism." This is misleading. Rolland insisted that it was a "constant state," not a transient experience. As he put it in his letter to Freud, "I myself am familiar with this sensation"; it was a "prolonged feeling" and "constant state (like a sheet of water which I feel flushing under the bark)."[76] Importantly, Freud himself understood it as such. By way of summarizing Rolland's letter in *Civilization and Its Discontents*, Freud notes that the oceanic feeling consists in a "peculiar feeling, which he himself is never without."[77] Freud, being an educated man and university professor well read in the classics, knew what the familiar transient mystical experience was and, as consequence, that Rolland's oceanic feeling could not be classified under that heading. Unfortunately, Freud was not familiar enough with the variety of mystical phenomena to know that permanent mystical states have been catalogued within religious traditions, as is evinced in the Hindu Sri Ramana Maharshi, who speaks of the prolonged feeling of the oceanic (as distinguished from the transient feeling of the oceanic, usually designated with the unqualified term *samadhi*) when describing the advanced mystical form known as *sahaja samadhi* (a qualified form of *samadhi*) and St. Teresa of

---

[75] See W. B. Parsons, *The Enigma of the Oceanic Feeling* (New York: Oxford University Press, 1999).

[76] Ibid., pp. 173–174.   [77] Ibid., p. 39.

Avila, who distinguished between transient unitive experiences (in Mansion Five of her mystical text *Interior Castle*) and the apex of the spiritual life (described in Mansion Seven) of the *spiritual marriage*, where the Holy Trinity resides permanently and continuously in the depths of the soul.[78] This is not to claim an exact equivalence between Rolland's oceanic feeling and those states described by St. Teresa and Sri Ramana Maharshi. Rather, it is to point out that the notion of a mystical state is not an anomaly; that other such mystical states exist.

In dealing with the state-like oceanic feeling, Freud's interpretative strategy emphasized preservation, not regression. He began by reflecting on what was for him new territory: the empirical, preoedipal developmental origin of such religious feelings. In the developmental stage of primary narcissism the infant's sense of self and the world is more unitary that that of the adult: "An infant at the breast does not as yet distinguish his ego from the external world as the source of the sensations flowing in upon him. He gradually learns to do so, in response to various promptings ... originally the ego includes everything, later it separates off an external world for itself."[79] He then goes on to conclude that adult ego-feelings are but a "shrunken residue" of an original all-embracing feeling and that there may exist many people in whose mental life this primary ego-feeling has persisted. If so, it "would exist in them side by side with the narrower and more sharply demarcated ego-feeling of maturity, like a kind of counterpart to it. In that case, the ideational content appropriate to it would be precisely those of limitlessness and of a bond with the universe – the same ideas with which my friend elucidated the 'oceanic feeling.'"[80] Freud went on to say that while in and of itself Rolland's oceanic feeling was neutral, akin to a developmental residue or psychological appendix, it could be taken up by the churches and framed in such a way as to cater to defensive modes of adapting to reality or, one might add, rekindle the memory of archaic, preoedipal forms of omnipotence and grandiosity.

As for the more familiar Jamesian episodic mystical experience, Freud ventured an opinion on that as well. This is most clearly seen in a paragraph in his *New Introductory Lectures* where Freud, responding to Rolland, contrasts mystical practices with the aim of psychoanalysis (i.e., what has been called the "psychoanalytic motto": where id was, there ego shall be). In this text Freud goes on to state: "It is easy to imagine ... that certain mystical practices may succeed in upsetting the normal relations between the different regions of the

---

[78] See A. Osborne, *Ramana Maharshi and the Path of Self-Knowledge* (New York: Samuel Weiser, 1973); St. Teresa of Avila, *The Interior Castle*. Trans. K. Kavanaugh and O. Rodriguez (New York: Paulist Press, 1979).
[79] Freud, *Civilization and Its Discontents*, S. E., vol. 21, pp. 66–67.   [80] Ibid.

mind, so that for instance, perception may be able to grasp happenings in the depths of the ego and in the id which were otherwise inaccessible to it."[81] While he goes on to say that "[i]t may safely be doubted . . . whether this road will lead us to the ultimate truths from which salvation is to be expected," he also admits "that the therapeutic efforts of psychoanalysis have chosen a similar line of approach."[82] In other words, Freud is drawing an equation between mystical techniques like yoga and psychoanalytic therapy. Freud admits that mystical practices, like psychoanalytic ones, help one dive into the depths of the unconscious, there to grasp the hidden, complex dynamics of the life of the unconscious. Where he draws the line is the further religious claim that such techniques help one access the "ultimate truths" that lead to "salvation." In other words, at best mystical practices can be in the service of gaining knowledge about unconscious contents which, if properly interpreted within the therapeutic situation, could be healing and adaptive.

This is carried further in another neglected text in Freud's correspondence with Rolland that deserves mention: his short, 1936 "open letter" (as he referred to it) to Rolland, written on the occasion of Rolland's sixtieth birthday and titled "A Disturbance of Memory on the Acropolis."[83] Freud framed the paper as a self-analytic session designed to explain the reason behind what he called a "feeling of derealization," one that led to a falsification of memory. The disturbance took place in 1904 during an annual trip he took with his brother Alexander. They had been planning to visit the Greek island of Corfu by way of the Italian port of Trieste. However, upon arriving in Trieste they were advised, due to inclement weather, to visit Athens instead. This option, says Freud, opened up the possible fulfillment of a long-standing wish to visit the Acropolis – a site rife with symbolism, pointing as it did to entry into the best of European culture. As such, it should have brought feelings of expectation, hope and pleasure. Instead, it brought a depressive and irresolute frame of mind that cast doubt on the feasibility of accomplishing the trip to Athens. When they finally did make it to Athens, Freud, standing amidst the ruins of the Acropolis, was astonished and moved to say: "So all this really does exist, just as we learnt at school!" He goes on to say that his utterance involved a "splitting of the ego" between the "person" who made the remark and the "person" who took cognizance of the remark. Whereas the first person was astonished at the existence of the Acropolis, the second person was astonished that the existence of the Acropolis was ever in doubt. Freud reasons that such a disturbance indicates

---

[81] This passage is from Freud's *New Introductory Lectures on Psychoanalysis*, S. E., vol. 22. For an extended discussion of the psychoanalytic motto and a deeper analysis of his views on mystical experience see W. B. Parsons, *Enigma of the Oceanic Feeling*.

[82] Ibid.   [83] Freud, "A Disturbance of Memory on the Acropolis," S. E., vol. 22, pp. 39–48.

he had a "feeling of derealization" that could be expressed as follows: "what I see here is not real."

Since the small paper is framed as an exercise in self-analysis, Freud went on to inquire as to what psychological forces were responsible for the derealization and, before that, his depressed mood upon learning he had an opportunity to go to Athens. Emphasizing the oedipal, Freud argued that his consternation was tied to the wish to "do better" than his father – a form of oedipal victory and success that invariably brought feelings of guilt:

> But here we come across the solution to the little problem of why it was that already at Trieste we interfered with our enjoyment of the voyage to Athens. It must be that a sense of guilt was attached to the satisfaction of having got so far: there was something about it that was wrong, that was from the earliest times forbidden ... It seems as though the essence of success were to have gotten further than one's father, and as though to excel one's father were something still forbidden.[84]

At Trieste, the fulfillment of the wish to go to Athens was only a possibility, leading to depression due to oedipal conflict. Once on the Acropolis, however, that possibility was turned into actuality: the wish was fulfilled. This unconscious wish was so powerful and forbidden that the ego had to resort to a new defense to ward off guilt, namely derealization: "what I see here is not real."

What, one may ask, does this have to do with Rolland and Eastern religions? By this point in time (1936) Rolland had sent him biographies of two saints, Ramakrishna and Vivekananda (published in 1930). Freud knew that the central tenets of Hinduism included Maya ("the world is an illusion") and reincarnation. As we have already seen, in *Civilization and Its Discontents* Freud was interested in finding out the "developmental infrastructure" of such doctrines. It was, then, feelings of derealization that were the basis of Maya – feelings that could be evoked though intense meditational activity, then misinterpreted by Hinduism as pertaining to the nature of reality. Along these lines it is relevant that in this "open letter" Freud also cast suspicion on reincarnation by stating that the phenomenon of déjà vu was "explained" by a "naively mystical and unpsychological attempt" to see in it "evidence of a former existence of our mental self." In other words, déjà vu was the true psychological core behind the (mistaken) doctrine of reincarnation. Finally, while Freud did not say so explicitly, one could extend his logic to posit a linked psychological phenomenon, the feeling of depersonalization (summarily put, the defensive thought "I am not real"), as the true psychological core of the (mistaken) mystical doctrine of the

---

[84] Ibid., p. 247.

illusory nature of the "self," best represented in the Buddhist doctrine of *anatta* (no self).

Freud offered two other important observations that merit our attention. First, while Freud wrote even less about Buddhism than he wrote about Hinduism, the little he did say has cast a lasting shadow on the psychoanalytic dialogue with Buddhism. Specifically, an almost off-the-cuff remark, in which Freud equated Thanatos with "the nirvana principle" (in his famous work *Beyond the Pleasure Principle* [1920]), has come to represent what is taken to be his rather disparaging view of Buddhism. By this Freud meant that while part of our instinctual constitution strives to make ever greater unities with others (i.e., Eros), its warring counterpart (Thanatos) is that which strives to reduce psychic tension, limit growth and complexity by compulsively repeating patterns of behavior and regressively actualizing an earlier inorganic state (i.e., death). Second, recalling our discussion in the previous section, the existential implication of this view becomes evident when, while commenting in *Civilization and Its Discontents* on the "programs for life" (i.e., ways of fulfilling happiness) as found in religious traditions, he mentions "the wisdom of the East." Freud goes on to suggest that, with respect to the latter, the path of the hermit is one option in that it adopts voluntary isolation in order to avoid suffering. In this sense, the worldly wisdom of the East prescribes that one "kill off the instincts," which, of course, is reminiscent of the death instinct. Needless to say, this was not Freud's stated preference (i.e., "to work and to love"). This is crucial, for while Freud was willing to say that Eastern introspective practices could lead to insights into the unconscious, he was also alerting the reader that such insights, if taken under the banner of religious ideology (the cultural superego), might prescribe taking those insights in the service of a "program for life" whose aims was at odds with the more rational aims of psychoanalysis.

Linking back to the portable lessons offered in *Civilization and It Discontents*, then, one could say that all of this indicates that Freud was doing for Eastern religions what he did for Western ones. Religious traditions that utilized doctrines like Maya, *anatta* and reincarnation were examples of the "unpsychological proceedings" of the (religious) cultural superego. As with Western religions, Freud offered a corrective concerning their doctrines: a developmental infrastructure that revealed their true psychological origins (e.g., derealization/depersonalization, déjà vu, Thanatos) while offering a better solution: a secular cure of souls designed to heighten the ability to (as Erik Erikson once put it) "leiben und arbeiten."[85]

---

[85] I have adapted this section from chapter 6 of my *Freud and Religion: Advancing the Dialogue*, which the interested reader may consult for more detail.

2 What Freud Got Wrong

Freud's views on monotheism were developed and applied not only in conjunction with clinical data and his own self-analysis but also as a result of his engagement with other academic disciplines. That said, his engagement with other social scientific work (anthropology and sociology) as well as theological and philosophical thought was not always met with favor. Disciplinary perspectives both outside and within psychoanalysis were quick to level decisive critiques that grew in sophistication through subsequent decades.

2.1 The Origins and Development of Religion

Freud's theory of the origin and development of religion has been thoroughly dismantled from numerous perspectives that can be subsumed under the following rubrics: *sources*, *biology*, *development* and *culture*.

One can start with his reliance on outdated and problematic *sources*. Freud never engaged in ethnographic research, instead relying on a group of anthropological theorists (e.g., E. B. Tylor, Sir James Frazer, Robertson Smith, J. J. Atkinson, Herbert Spencer) labeled the "armchair titans," signifying their lack of personal ethnographic work and questionable reliance on data supplied by missionaries, travelers and others on the ground. Yet even in Freud's own day the theories of such anthropologists were subject to critiques that would render them problematic. As one pundit put it, their conclusions "had been rejected by the anthropological profession before *Totem and Taboo* reached it."[86] What, then, were the dubious conclusions Freud adopted as probable or true? For one, while the term "totemism," despite being a Western colonialist construct, was admitted to having existed in some form in some cultures, it was disputed that it was a unitary phenomenon with stable characteristics. Among the latter Freud took as valid are the following: (1) the framing of totemism as not only universal but also the earliest form of religion; (2) the notion that totemism was necessarily linked with exogamy and the prohibition against killing; (3) the actual existence of the totem meal; (4) the universality of the primal horde and the enactment of patricide (the primal deed). In sum, Freud's argument was seen as built on scholarly sand.

Turning to *biology*, we have seen that Freud promoted the view that humanity, as a collective, was possessed of an "archaic heritage," a phylogenetically inculcated oedipal dynamic. Unfortunately for Freud, Lamarck's thesis had been disputed as early as the 1880s by the biologist August Weismann while Ernst Haeckel's recapitulation theory was discredited with the emergence of

---

[86] E. Wallace, *Freud and Anthropology* (New York: International Universities Press, 1983), p. 113.

genetics as the reigning theory of transmission.[87] As a result, one could no longer hold that physical and cultural characteristics acquired during the course of a lifetime could be genetically transmitted. Freud's attempt to situate Oedipus as a foundational "universal archetype," hence the driver of all religious formations, was dependent on discredited theories. One can conclude that Oedipus is not the root and key to human civilization, religion and morality; the nineteenth-century socio-evolutionary thesis and its implications do not hold and there is no "phylogenetic unconscious" that is dynamic and the determining factor in manifesting cultural forms favoring patriarchy and monotheism.

In the specific case of Judaism and Moses, additional critiques are found. Historians and biblical scholars have vented at the sheer number of Freud's historical mistakes and dependence on outdated and questionable sources.[88] For example, Moses may be an Egyptian name, but there is no evidence that he was anything but a Hebrew. Additionally, Freud's portrait of the Egyptian pharaoh Akhenaten as a reformer who instituted monotheism is an error, as is the notion that ethics was at its core.[89] The latter did not offer "ethical discipline in the formation of character" and evinced "no interest in social justice or the welfare of society."[90] There is, then, "no basis for a conclusion that Akhenaten's Atonism was the inspiration for Mosaic monotheism."[91] The postulation of "two Moseses" (Egyptian, Midianite) remains unsubstantiated and Ernst Sellin, the scholar Freud depended on for his thesis that Moses was murdered, came to doubt, if not formally retract, his own hypothesis (to which Freud predictably responded: "it might be true all the same"[92]). The psychoanalyst W. W. Meissner, by way of summarizing the findings of contemporary biblical scholarship, was able to conclude: "Freud was able to advance an ingenious reconstruction on the basis of a historical account that has so altered in the intervening years that it is no longer tenable."[93]

To be clear, those in contemporary psychoanalysis are more than willing to discard Freud's myth of origins, phylogenesis and historical development. Even so, a further round of *cultural* critiques requires a different revision of psychoanalytic theory, especially as regards his view of ontogenetic *development*. This is so for even if one discards Freud's theory of origins one could still hold to the universality of the Oedipus complex. Yet even in Freud's day anthropologists and psychoanalysts alike felt compelled to offer cultural counters to Freud's

---

[87] Ibid., p. 64.

[88] See, for example, W. F. Albright's classic work *From the Stone Age to Christianity* (Baltimore, MD: Johns Hopkins Press, 1946), pp. 166–167, 194–196.

[89] See E. Rice, *Freud and Moses* (Albany: State University Press of New York, 1990), p. 139.

[90] Ibid., pp. 139–140.   [91] Ibid., p. 141.   [92] Ibid., p. 149.

[93] See W. W. Meissner, *Psychoanalysis and Religious Experience* (New Haven, CT: Yale University Press, 1986), pp. 108ff.

universalism. For example, the anthropologist Bronislaw Malinowski documented that certain cultures did not evince the oedipal triangle.[94] Again, two of Freud's non-Western psychoanalytic correspondents, the Hindu Girindrasekhar Bose and the Buddhist Heisaku Kosawa, both of whom were instrumental in founding psychoanalytic institutes in India and Japan respectively, also argued that different kinds of "complexes" not named Oedipus were found in their clinics.[95]

After Freud's death, the debate over universality and attendant cultural issues achieved a new level of reflexive sophistication. While the critiques and counters offered by those in both the anthropological and the psychoanalytic professions differed in specific detail, they agreed on several general conclusions: (1) Oedipus is better framed as a universal possibility but not a universal actuality, which means its actualization is dependent on certain family and cultural configurations. (2) Freud is better cast as a psychologically gifted ethnographer of his culture who unfortunately went to great lengths to universalize (and then "ground" historically in *Totem and Taboo*) a local sociohistorical finding with only a narrow, selected sample size. (3) Culture "gets into" the mind not only through the superego, as Freud claimed, but also into the ego (the "what" of reality is mediated by culture) and the id (culture "patterns" the expression of aggressive/sexual impulses through the mother–infant relationship). (4) culture shapes the length and importance of each developmental phase (the obvious example being that of adolescence). (5) Different cultures valorize different "defense mechanisms" as well as facilitate different forms of neuroses.[96] These conclusions meant that, going forward, psychoanalytic models need to be reformed and adapted to each and every new culture, which amounts to the injunction that psychoanalysis must engage its sister social sciences as equal partners in the task of interpretation.

A further, related series of critiques centered on the ethno-psychological elements buried in what Freud framed as the supposed value-neutral "scientific" theory he offered to culture at large. In particular, feminist and critical race theories have labored to unveil the normative (i.e., "culturally coded") views of race and gender found in *Totem and Taboo*. The assumed developmental trajectory of women and people of color is especially problematic when combined with the anthropological literature Freud favored in that the latter

---

[94] B. Malinowski, *Sex and Repression in Savage Society* (London: Forgotten Books, 2012 [1927]).

[95] This does not obviate the possibility, as I argue following R. Paul, that a culture may be organized with an oedipal gradient (see my *Freud and Religion*, ch's 2 and 3, especially p. 90, ft. 35).

[96] Freud once wrote that "every neurosis has a purpose: it is directed toward certain persons and would disappear at once on a South Sea island or in a similar situation for there would be no longer a reason for it" (see E. Wallace, *Freud and Anthropology*, p. 185).

promoted a socio-evolutionary perspective on the nature and history of human civilizations. Again, by the time Freud was writing *Totem and Taboo*, their general socio-evolutionary perspective on civilization had been thoroughly critiqued and, to a large extent, discredited. Indeed, the ethnocentrism baked into the supposedly value-neutral and scientific postulates of evolutionary "stages" and "hierarchies" complete with value-laden notions of race, ethnicity and "the primitive" had been firmly exposed and dismantled. The subsequent anthropological rejection of socio-evolutionism avowed that there was no progression from barbarism to civilization, no biological variations between races, no "higher or lower" in civilization, and more: "all men are totally civilized."[97]

The deeper problem is that if one links the thought of Lamarck and anthropological socio-evolutionism with psychoanalytic concepts like regression, fixation, primitivity and developmental stages, and both under the banner of assuming white male European civilization as the highest evolved standard (as did Freud), then one is in danger of unjustly framing "the Other" as less individuated, moral, intelligent and prone to "primary process" functioning. Moreover, this "Other" can take multiple forms: women, people of color and religious traditions. To illustrate this, one can turn to two of the original members of the Indian psychoanalytic society, Owen Berkeley-Hill and Claude Danger Daly, who, in using psychoanalysis as a vehicle of cultural oppression and British colonialism, portrayed Indians as infantile and inferior.[98] Daly, for example, wrote that "in the Hindu one finds a psychology that differs considerably from the European, its equivalent with us being found in pathological cases."[99] Fittingly, Salman Akhtar (a contemporary Indian-American psychoanalyst) refers to this as "a racist countertransference."[100] Such notions extended to the clinical encounter, as is evinced in psychoanalytic case histories of African-Americans in the prestigious journal *Psychoanalytic Quarterly* in 1914 (and here the authors, following Freud, assumed the biogenic law in which individual development recapitulates "the history of the race"), where such patients were framed as less individuated, more prone to regression, psychosis, and primary process thought, and lacking in ego-strength.[101]

---

[97] The phrase was uttered by F. Boaz. See Wallace, *Freud and Anthropology*, pp. 64–65.

[98] S. Aktar and P. Tummala-Narra, "Psychoanalysis in India," in S. Aktar (ed.), *Freud along the Ganges* (New Delhi: Stanza, 2008), pp. 11–12.

[99] Ibid.   [100] Ibid., p. 13.

[101] C. Brickman, *Aboriginal Populations in the Mind* (New York: Columbia University Press, 2003), p. 87. There has been a robust literature on how to preform reflexive applied psychoanalysis with regard to race. F. Fanon's *Black Skin, White Masks* (New York: Grove Press, 2008 [1952]) was, of course, the classic original work in this field. For more contemporary representative studies see, for example, E. Abel, "Race, Class, and Psychoanalysis? Opening Questions," in M. Hirsch and E. F. Keller (eds.), *Conflicts in Feminism* (New York:

While *Totem and Taboo* did not specifically articulate a theoretical position with respect to female development, scholars have linked Freud's later essays on the latter to his views on what he called "primitives." Early feminist responses to Freud's views on development, most forcefully instituted by Simone de Beauvoir's *The Second Sex* (1949), were prelude to the eventual consensus even within the psychoanalytic establishment that Freud failed to appreciate the influence of culture on psychological development. He collapsed culture and psychological development, thereby not allowing space for culture to be a partner in determining how women develop. Freud simply assumed that the cultural construction of what it meant to be male and female in all cultures is invariant and essential.

Fortunately a robust body of literature exists that affords a corrective to the cautionary tales we have elaborated – a corrective that seeks to revise, without wholly abandoning, psychoanalytic methodology. For example, Diane Jonte-Pace, in summarizing the history of critiques emanating from both feminist and race perspectives, suggests that they can be framed as falling into three basic groupings: critical, inclusive and analytic.[102] Critical theorists tend to dismiss Freud altogether; inclusivists tend to move from Freud to other, less overtly racist/misogynist psychologies; analytic theorists (initiated by Franz Fanon's *Black Skin, White Masks* and Juliet Mitchell's *Psychoanalysis and Feminism*) not only advocate for cultural reflexivity and the reformation of "ethno" assumptions within psychoanalytic theory but also promote a culturally self-reflexive form of psychoanalysis as methodologically useful. It does so by showing how psychoanalysis can illumine the way in which cultures manifest and maintain their unequal gendered hierarchies and racist elements. Rather than reproducing social norms, a reflexive psychoanalysis can illumine, challenge and deconstruct them. Properly revised, "applied" psychoanalysis is all the more helpful in analyzing the implicit assumptions concerning race and gender in religious narratives and practices. They point to a general portable

---

Routledge, 1990), pp. 184–204; J. Lorand, *The Fetish Revisited: Marx, Freud, and the Gods Black People Make* (Durham, NC: Duke University Press, 2018).

[102] See the following works of D. Jonte-Pace : "Analysts, Critics, and Inclusivists: Feminist Voices in the Psychology of Religion," in D. Jonte-Pace and W. B. Parsons (eds.)., *Religion and Psychology: Mapping the Terrain* (New York: Routledge, 2001), pp. 129–148; "Psychoanalysis, Colonialism, and Modernity: Reflections on Brickman's *Aboriginal Populations in the Mind, Religious Studies Review* 32(1), 2006, 1–4; *Speaking the Unspeakable* (Berkeley: University of California Press, 2001). For further representative studies on how psychoanalysis can reflexively engage constructions of sexuality and gender, see J. Mitchell, *Psychoanalysis and Feminism* (New York: Basic Books, 2000 [1974]); N. Chodorow, *The Reproduction of Mothering* (Berkeley: University of California Press, 1978); J. Hamman, "The Reproduction of the Hypermasculine Male: Select Subaltern Views." *Pastoral Psychology* 66, 2017, 799–818.

lesson: when one uses psychoanalytic methodology to analyze religious phe-nomena, it is better to do so in dialogue with the perspectives offered by its sister social sciences and culture theorists. Taking a cue from this body of literature, then, we can refer to such a dialogue as evincing the trait of *reflexivity*. Through such dialogue psychoanalytic models are reformed and clarified, reductionism and Orientalism (i.e., the employment of stereotypical narratives designed to maintain Western colonial power) mitigated, "ethno" elements made transpar-ent and manifest errors avoided.

2.2 Freud and Contemporary Religions

There has also been an abundance of scholarly critique of Freud's commentary on contemporary religions. Their diversity can be organized with respect to the following rubrics: (1) the definitional problem with respect to his use of the term "religion"; (2) responses from religious intellectuals; (3) social scientific objec-tions to his adherence to the fact of secularization; (3) observations from feminist and race theorists concerning his continued lack of cultural reflexivity; (4) later psychoanalytic critiques.

2.3 The Definitional Debate

As we have seen, Freud's interests were focused on Western religious traditions, assumed institutionalized patriarchal forms of sociocultural power and valorized normative expressions centered on the monotheistic "mighty personality" of an exalted Father-God. Freud further qualified this as pertaining to the understanding of religion found in the "common-man." It is clear, then, how Freud entered what we have called the "definitional debate" as regards religion. The question is how to evaluate his strategy. With respect to those working in the discipline of religious studies as a whole, Freud's position raises multiple concerns if taken to apply to the entire territory of the "what" of religion. Even a cursory survey of the history of method spanning theological, philosophical, anthropological and sociological approaches reveals multiple and often contested ways of defining religion. Properly qualified, there is a place for Freud's definition of religion as well as his model for interpreting it. There may be some for whom the oedipally based common-man's religion is an approximate fit, and one can admit to the general observation that, regardless of how one defines religion, any faith journey carries with it the "baggage" of some form of developmental determinism. At the same time, if by "religion" we mean a cultural phenomenon that admits of being empirically wider, more culturally complex and theologically informed than that addressed by Freud, then at the very least a certain interdisciplinary dialogue is needed, if only to see where Freud's interpretative efforts are of value.

2.4 Religious Counters

A good deal of such interdisciplinary dialogue has taken place through the auspices of religious intellectuals working within what have been called the *psychology–theology dialogue* and the *psychology–comparativist dialogue*.[103] While we cannot address the responses of each and every one of the figures that populate these dialogues they can, as we will shortly see, be understood as finding their origins with respect to multiple correspondents of Freud.

To make clear a central difference between Freud and the responses from religious intellectuals, we can utilize the following metaphors. Freud's theory of religion can be likened to a movie. The (dis)contents of one's psyche are projected onto the cultural "screen" in the disguised and distorted form known as "religion," only to be retranslated and reinterpreted in light of theories about its proper source (i.e., the human imagination). In the case of Freud the projector responsible for the religious movie seen by the audience on the cultural screen will always follow the laws of his theory. Whether dealing with the origins, rituals or everyday religiosity of the common-man, Freud will see elements of the structural model, developmental considerations, fathers and Oedipus everywhere. For religious intellectuals operating within the afore-mentioned dialogues the fundamental fault of this methodological perspective, if taken to apply to the entire territory of what constitutes religion, is that it is *reductive*. As a counter, religious intellectuals who have engaged Freud favor an astronomical metaphor. For example, take seeing a bright star on a clear night. Let's say that the star represents the Light of the divine, whatever you may consider that to be. If you were a theologian or a religious believer of any kind, you would insist that the Light "is." While insisting on the reality of the star, theologians sympathetic to Freud are willing to admit that one's relation to the Light may well be refracted by the Earth's atmosphere and by the perspective of the observer (which is to say, by the very human developmental and cultural "baggage" we carry along for the ride). This is a necessary task for, once understood and clarified, the believer's religion to the Light is shorn, to the extent possible, of that baggage. In that way religious intellectuals are apt to embrace Freud yet also theorize how one can go beyond atmospherics to the reality of the Light as found in the person of faith. In so doing, their conceptual strategies fall along the following general rubrics: (1) an alternate definition of religion; (2) a corresponding non-oedipally based understanding of the divine; (3) alternate framings of the human personality that, in taking into account Freud's structural model, might add enough nuance to enable the possibility for a faith journey that transcends developmental determinants (in Western terms,

---

[103] See D. Jonte-Pace and W.B. Parsons, eds., *Religion and Psychology*.

this is the category of "theological anthropology"). The consequences are logical to predict: if one offers a different definitional strategy that is linked to an expanded view of the person and a framing of the divine that transcends the determinants of the earthly father, then one can arrive at a view of the faith journey that is better suited to the "star" metaphor than the "movie" metaphor.

To illustrate this with respect to Western religious intellectuals it will suffice to take but one example: Freud's long relationship with Oskar Pfister, a Protestant pastor who eventually became one of the first lay analysts. Shortly after writing *The Future of an Illusion* Freud sent a copy to Pfister, who responded with a short essay entitled "The Illusion of a Future."[104] It is in the latter that the conceptual strategies discussed herein can be found. For example, while Pfister agreed that "ideas of God and the beyond are often painted with colours from a wish-palette" and, on a personal level, he found in his own faith journey "the features of my father, of various pastors ... and behind them the direction of hatred," he also considered it "wrong to squeeze all rejections of religion into a wish-schema."[105] Signifying his own entry into the definitional debate, Pfister stated that "[i]t is a great shame that Freud neglects the very highest expressions of religion" and, further (in a letter to Freud): "our difference derives chiefly from the fact that you grew up in proximity to pathological forms of religion and regard these as 'religion,' while I had the good fortune of being able to turn to a free form of religion which to you seems to be an emptying of Christianity of its content, while I regard it as the core and substance of religion."[106] In other words, tallying with what we referred to as the star metaphor, Pfister was declaring that in his view projected oedipal elements are only one part of a total quilt of one's representation of the divine. Pfister went on to define his own conception of the divine as "one which, based on the first chapter of the Gospel of St. John, I regard as divine wisdom and love."[107]

In order to embrace Freud yet also go beyond him to articulate a faith journey that is only partially determined by developmental considerations Pfister had to articulate a new conception of the person (theological anthropology). He thus offered the figure of Jesus as well as selected figures in Protestant theology as illustrations of his point. For example, the "religion" Jesus advocated corresponded to a view of human nature Pfister described as an "ideal-realism" based on "a magnificent, intuitive anthropology and cosmology."[108] This new conception of the person allowed Pfister to claim that Jesus' ideas of "the father"

---

[104] O. Pfister, "The Illusion of the Future: A Friendly Disagreement with Prof. Sigmund Freud." *International Journal of Psychoanalysis* 74 (1993), 557–579.

[105] Ibid., p. 563.

[106] Ibid., p. 562; H. Meng and E.L. Freud, eds., *Psychoanalysis and Faith*, p. 122.

[107] Ibid., p. 578.   [108] Ibid., p. 564.

were "completely cleansed of the dross of oedipal attachment [and] heteronomy."[109] In turn, Pfister framed Jesus as championing what could retrospectively be called a pastoral form of psychoanalysis. Jesus handled "transference" in a way that "deserved the admiration of all Freud's pupils," dissolving the oedipal complex and raising the individual to a higher moral plane.[110] He could do so, claimed Pfister, because, unlike the common-man's religion, Jesus valorized "coercion-free individualism" and aimed at a higher form of love in which "everything egotistical disappears."[111] The basic structural elements Pfister laid down are portable, found in the more sophisticated theological responses (the details and content of which vary) in later figures such as Paul Tillich, Paul Ricoeur, Don Browning, and James Fowler.[112]

Turning to those engaged in countering Freud with respect to Eastern religions, one finds the same general principles (i.e., the star metaphor, the three strategies) being employed. One can find the initial salvos in Freuds relationship with three central correspondents who defended Hinduism and Buddhism: the disillusioned Catholic Romain Rolland, the Indian psychoanalyst Girindreasakar Bose and the Japanese analyst Heisaku Kosawa. Like their counterparts in the *psychology–theology* dialogue, all three shared the general complaint concerning Freud's definitional strategy, even if they specified the "what" of religion differently. It would be fair to say that the three men thought that Freud's contribution was limited to what we can call the "common-man's" Hinduism and Buddhism and that the wisdom of Eastern religions contained a deeper dimension that transcended such developmental determinants. Again, like their aforementioned counterparts, they linked new definitional strategies to alternate conceptions of the person (i.e., theological anthropology) and the divine.

In the case of Rolland, his request to Freud was that he investigate the oceanic feeling in the hopes that a "mystical psychoanalysis" might result. He affirmed the latter in his biographies of the Hindu saints by stating that he was convinced that the theories of the "modern psycho-physiologist" would be eventually able to harness the wisdom of mysticism. He agreed with Freud's view of mystical practices like Yoga up to a point. As he colloquially put it, the "ancient Yogis did not wait for Dr. Freud to teach them that the best cure for the mind is to make it look its deeply hidden monsters straight in the face."[113] He framed Yoga as a "science of the soul" that helped one gain access to and mastery of unconscious contents. On the other hand, Rolland found psychoanalytic analyses of

---

[109] Ibid., p. 561.   [110] Ibid., p. 562.   [111] Ibid., p. 564.

[112] For more detail on these figures and their responses to psychoanalysis, see W.B. Parsons, *Freud and Religion*, ch. 4.

[113] W.B. Parsons, *Enigma of the Oceanic Feeling*, p. 67.

mysticism limited. So it is, in differing from Freud, Rolland posited that the ultimate aim of Yoga was to help one access even deeper layers of the unconscious. In so doing, he explicitly engaged one of the Jamesian "marks" of mystical experience – *noesis* (i.e., mystical claims to knowledge) – framing it as the central problem of mysticism. Indeed, like James, Rolland entered into the definitional debate about religion by claiming that the deepest core and origin of religion lay in mysticism. Rolland understood that in dealing with complex matters of mystical epistemology one had to engage the ruling philosophical figure of Immanuel Kant, who had argued the impossibility of truly knowing the divine (the *noumena*) given the conditions and limits of human cognition. Without providing any compelling philosophical arguments, Rolland nevertheless claimed that "centuries before Kant" various Indian philosophers "had already predicated and even surpassed" his limited view. The secret, thought Rolland, lay in a cognitive faculty he termed mystical "intuition" that, accessed and developed through Yoga, enabled one to transcend individual consciousness and merge with the Absolute.[114] Therein lay an impasse between him and Freud that never went beyond this initial stage.

Freud's correspondence with Girindrasekhar Bose (1887–1953), who eventually became the primary advocate of psychoanalysis in India, ran from 1921 to 1937, comprised close to two dozen letters, and was virtually concurrent with his correspondence with Rolland (1923–1939).[115] Bose received his medical degree from Calcutta Medical College (1910) and received the first doctor of science degree awarded in India (1921) for his doctoral thesis titled *The Concept of Repression*. By 1922 Bose had helped found the first Indian psychoanalytic society in Calcutta, beginning a fruitful history of Indian psychoanalysts, not the least of which include S. C. Mitra and Tarun Sinha, successive presidents of the Indian Psychoanalytic Society after Bose's death, and Sudhir Kakar, a prominent student of Erik Erikson and the leading contemporary Indian psychoanalyst.

Bose argued for an addition to Freud's structural model: a grand metapsychological concept he dubbed the "theoretical ego." The latter targets "the average man's 'I' that feels the continuity of experience" and, as such, can be said to be the "hypothetical entity which maintains the continuity of mental experience both conscious and unconscious ... the thread which keeps the individual beads together in a necklace."[116] As such, the theoretical ego is

---

[114] Ibid., ch. 3.
[115] For a comprehensive overview and analysis of the Freud–Bose correspondence see A. Hiltebeitel, *Freud's India: Sigmund Freud and India's First Psychoanalyst, Girindrasekhar Bose* (New York: Oxford University Press, 2018).
[116] Ibid., p. 114.

"the great reservoir of all wishes both conscious and unconscious. It includes within itself the Freudian ego, the id, and the super-ego, in fact, all manifest-ations of mental life."[117] Bose, who had an allegiance to the Upanishads and Advaita Vedanta, seems to have imported Hindu philosophy into the notion of a theoretical ego. As Hiltebeitel notes, the latter embodies the characteristics of a *jivatman* (a "living Self") and employs Hindu images in its description: "[Bose's] Vedanta-oriented readers and patients could recognize it as synonym-ous with the *jivatman*: the self caught up in *samsaric* life that would nonetheless be theoretically (ontologically and 'ultimately') free not only from reincarna-tion caused by karmic suffering, but from biological drives."[118]

Bose formally articulated this transformational position in a small paper titled "The Psychological Outlook of Hindu Philosophy," delivered at the Indian Philosophical Congress in 1930. This paper can be framed as Bose's Hindu counterpart to Pfister's Protestant response to Freud as contained in his "The Illusion of the Future." Entering the definitional debate, Bose was willing to admit, as had Pfister, to a form of religion where God is a projection and designed to cater to infantile needs. He sees this "social type" encoded in the Bhagavad Gita, where one finds those who "believe" due to personal needs, external dangers and, as a result, creates "God out of his own mental image."[119] That said, he also argued that psychoanalysis needed to recognize the poten-tially adaptive value of religion: "religion served as a palliative for human suffering and was deemed therefore 'practical' for Bose rather than as the obsessive, collective neurosis that it was for Freud."[120] Then, however, in going even further, he offered the example of the Upanishads, framed as a higher, introspective and psychological form of religion. Here the religious seeker is redefined as bound not by feelings of need and danger but by the need for wisdom. This kind of person asks pertinent and sophisticated psychological questions, such as "how do dreams arise?" and "which is the agent in the body that feels pleasure?"[121] In asking such questions, and employing different introspective techniques such as Yoga to find their answers, the early Upanishadic *rishis* accessed a deeper level of consciousness, termed by Bose "pure consciousness" (consciousness without an object), which had the thera-peutic effect of leading to a condition in which "all pains cease to exist, and there is a peculiar feeling of blissfulness."[122] In a psychoanalytic reframing of the Upanishadic claim that the meditative insight into Brahman results in "Sat, Chit, Ananda" (Truth, [pure] Consciousness, Bliss), Bose was offering a Hindu

---

[117] Ibid.   [118] Ibid., p. 119.

[119] G. Bose, "The Psychological Outlook of Hindu Philosophy," *Indian Journal of Psychology* 5, 1930, 119–146.

[120] Ibid., p. 126.   [121] Ibid., pp. 125–126.   [122] Ibid., p. 133.

variant of Rolland's desire to see the establishment of a "mystical psychoanalysis." Indeed, both Rolland and Bose prefigured what we will shortly see as the development of what has been dubbed the "transformational" school of psychoanalysis.[123]

The third important figure in the emergence of the psychology–comparativist dialogue was the Buddhist Heisaku Kosawa (1897–1968), often referred to as the "father" of Japanese psychoanalysis and the first president of the Japan Psychoanalytical Association. Kosawa was intrigued enough with Freud's ideas that, from 1931 to 1933, he took it upon himself to travel to Vienna, there to receive a personal analysis with Richard Sterba, one of Freud's colleagues, further being trained by Paul Federn, another one of Freud's colleagues, for the purpose of legitimating his status as a full-fledged analyst. He met with Freud (he said he loved the "sitting Buddha" in front of the bookshelf in Freud's study), engaged in a correspondence with him, even sent him as a gift a portrait of Mount Fuji (which still graces a wall in the Freud Museum in London). Kosawa returned to Japan to set up his own practice, claiming that Japanese patients were best served by Japanese analysts.

In order to understand how Kosawa countered Freud's views on religion one must first provide a brief summary of the nature of his Buddhist leanings. Brought up in a household harboring only a trace of Buddhism, things changed for Kosawa in his early twenties when he encountered Chikazumi Jokan (1870–1941), a monk in the tradition of Pure Land (Jodo Shinshu) Buddhism, and the writings of Shinran, its thirteenth-century Japanese founder. Pure Land traces its origins back to India, later traveling to China and then Japan, valorizing the Mahayana values of compassion for others and devotion to the saving power of the Amitabha Buddha (a "transcendent" divinity who had created a heavenly Pure Land to which adherents would travel after death). Mediated through Shinran and Jokan, Kosawa became enamored of the Pure Land distinction between *jiriki* (the power of the individual to save oneself) and *tariki* (the saving power of the Other, in this case, Amitaba). For Kosawa it was *tariki* that finally held sway to the point that a signature insight of life was to realize the fact of one's weakness, frailty, defilements and complete inability to manufacture enlightenment. So it is that Kosawa emphasized *shinjin* or "true entrusting," that moment in which one realizes that because one is incapable of procuring salvation by oneself one must turn to the Other (again being the compassion and grace of Amitaba). Even here one comes to understand that such faith is not part of the human equipment but due to Amitabha reaching out in love ("The voice with which I call Amida

---

[123] See W.B. Parsons, *Enigma of the Oceanic Feeling*.

Buddha/Is the voice with which Amida Buddha calls to me").[124] The realiza-
tion of Amitaba's unconditional love, grace and saving power despite one's
defilements led to a specific character change: the "melting" of resistance and
anger, the turn to repentance and, as a result, the overwhelming gratitude for
being unconditionally accepted and loved. While the comparison is oversim-
plified, one can at least see how some scholars have drawn affinities between
this characterization of Pure Land Buddhism and Protestant Christianity.

Kosawa parlayed his differences with Freud into a critique of the latter's
views on religion. For example, entering as those before him into definitional
debates about religion, he claimed that *Totem and Taboo* was not aimed at
a "unified" state of the religious mind and hence not "really" about an analysis
of religion at all. *Future of an Illusion*, based on Oedipus and its attendant
emotions of fear and guilt, was also not a "true" form of religion. Rather, "true
religion with a unified state of mind" was best exemplified in Shinran, Jokan and
Pure Land Buddhism. Moreover, the realized aim of Buddhism and its greatest
figures, constituted by the melting of hatred and guilt into heartfelt repentance,
gratitude and compassion, was precisely that which psychoanalysis could help
to facilitate. Again, fiddling with definitions of what "being religious" means,
Kosawa held that it is this framing of a successful therapeutic intervention that
was held up as a "religious state of mind." Buddhism and psychoanalysis, then,
were wholly compatible. As he put it: "I cannot help but compare Dr. Freud's
mindset with that of St. Shinran."[125]

2.5 Sociological Reservations

As previously noted, Freud entered the debate not only over how to define
religion but also over how to define secularization, insisting on a strong
version of the "decline" theory. Existing literature on the topic cautions that
any assessment of the reality of secularization is inexorably linked with how
one defines religion.[126] For example, proponents of the decline theory often
define religion as Western, institutional and implicitly Christian and, as
a result, link what they think is the fact of secularization with numerous causes
(e.g., pluralism, modernity, class stratification, separation of church and state,

---

[124] C. Harding, I. Fumiaki and Y. Shin'ichi (eds.), *Religion and Psychotherapy in Modern Japan*
(New York: Routledge, 1995), chs. 1 and 5.

[125] Ibid., p. 123.

[126] As the anthropologist Mary Douglas once put it, any debate over the reality of secularization
"due to modernization" is entirely dependent on one's "chosen definition of religion" (see
M. Douglas, "The Effects of Modernization on Religious Change," in M. Douglas and
S. Tipton, eds., *Religion and America: Spiritual Life in a Secular Age* [Boston, MA: Beacon
Press, 1982, p. 30]). Other prominent social theorists (e.g., T. Luckmann, C. Bender, L.
Woodhead) have made similar points.

democracy, privatization and the rise of individualism). If one grants this definitional strategy of what constitutes "religion" and "secularization," there may be some truth to the reality of religious decline (paradigmatically articulated by Peter Berger in his classic work *The Sacred Canopy*). However, even here the decline is local, not universal, and history has seen reversals, again paradigmatically stated by Peter Berger who, having once sided with the decline theorists, later admitted that he had been mistaken.[127] Along these lines it is the case that Christianity in the southern hemisphere and Islam globally are on the rise, not decline. Further, if one changes up one's definition of religion to include unchurched, noninstitutional cultural expressions, para-digmatically seen in the rapid contemporary growth of those whom profess to be "Nones," "New Age" or "Spiritual but Not Religious," one sees once again not only the "persistence" of religion and spirituality but its growth.[128] In sum, there are no indications that Freud's prediction that religion would entirely disappear is correct. This does not mean that his program for creating a social space for psychoanalysis, as a secular cure of souls, is not an advance for civilization. One can still use Freud and his advocacy of a secular cure of souls without endorsing his simple conclusions regarding secularization. Certainly psychoanalysis has become not only a legitimate secular cure of souls but has also made its way well past the clinic to universities, to the arts and even political systems, there to be used as a tool for investigation and interpretation, and an aid in the project of social structural change and individual transformation.

2.6 Feminist and Race Critiques

Feminists and race theorists have seen *Future of an Illusion* marred by the same lack of cultural reflexivity found in *Totem and Taboo*. As in the latter, Freud continued his evolutionary views of comparative human societies in which "contemporary" religion (now described with the unfortunate choice of words as "our present-day white Christian civilization") is seen as bearing a "fatal resemblance to the mental products of primitive peoples," thereby drawing an analogy between the regressed, childish neurotic believer (the common-man) and "the primitive."[129] Similarly, feminists have noted how Freud's view of gender crept into his analysis of the regressed, childish believer. In contrast to

---

[127] See P. Berger, *Sacred Canopy* (New York: Anchor Books, 1990[1967]). For his retraction, see www.christiancentury.org/article/2012-03/protestantism-and-quest-certainty.

[128] See, for example, W. B. Parsons (ed.), *Being Spiritual but Not Religious: Past, Present, Futures* (New York: Routledge, 2018); E. Drescher, *Choosing Our Religion: The Spiritual Lives of America's Nones* (New York: Oxford, 2016).

[129] C. Brickman, *Aboriginal Populations in the Mind*, p. 46.

the common-man, Freud posits the normative ideal of the mature, "post-religious" brainworker who subscribes to the gods of reason (*Logos*, now read as science) and brute necessity (*Ananke*, the fact of the natural, amoral world of cause and effect). As noted earlier, such an individual is characterized as individuated, as without illusions, as capable of introspection and sublimation and as having a healthy superego. But those utilizing the resources of gender theory have noted that this portrait tallies with Freud's views of the ideal, mature male while his characterization of the believer is more like his view of femininity: "both believers and women share common psychical characteristics: a weak super-ego, a poorly developed sense of morality, a restricted intellect, opposition to cultural advance, insufficient respect for reality, *Ananke* and *Logos*."[130] Freud depends on masculinity as the universal norm and ideal while his analysis assumes a patricentric, patriarchal culture and a form of religion situated within it.

Such cautionary tales do not abrogate his many insights or the proper application of his models so much as ask us to perform the needed reflexive acts to shear psychoanalytic models of unnecessary linkages for proper use. As recounted earlier, some feminist and critical race approaches, while discarding Freud's essentialism with regard to gender, race, and the primitive, reframe his analysis as profitable if taken to be a deconstructive act that illuminates the structure of patriarchal culture, structural racism and its attendant religious forms. If utilized in this way, psychoanalysis can be used as a powerful means of socioreligious critique.

2.7 Later Psychoanalytic Revisions

As one might imagine, post-Freudian psychoanalytic theorizing in general incorporates a vast spectrum of figures and models. As a result, one must narrate that history with respect to its influence on specifically psychoanalytic theorizing about religion in a selective fashion. Choices have to be made, and our selection is based on those figures that best represent advances, nodal points as it were, in that evolution.

In beginning, then, later psychoanalytic revisions of Freud's theorizing about religion fall into three camps: (1) ego psychological, (2) object relational and (3) transformational.[131] The first two revised and expanded Freud's views on the ego. In theorizing about the ego Freud established two intersecting models: (1) the ego as a "mechanism" (e.g., repression, sublimation, regression, projection, etc.) which functioned to defend against unwanted unconscious drives while helping one adapt to external reality; (2) the ego as the repository of what Freud referred to

---

[130] Ibid., p. 123.   [131] I take the survey in this section from my *Freud and Religion*, ch. 7.

as "abandoned object-cathexis," which in experience-near language amounts to the felt sense of I or Self. The latter was conceived by Freud as being built up in part of idealizations and identifications with loved "objects" like one's parents and significant others. Over the course of development, previously loved and idealized objects (persons) are partially left behind (which is to say, "deidealized"), as is the norm during the process of maturation. At the same time, such identifications are internalized and memorialized as part of one's own psychological structure (i.e., one's ideals, values, aims and pursuits). These two lines of ego theorizing, then, became the theoretical basis for the development of ego psychology (as found in theorists like Anna Freud, Erik Erikson, Heinz Hartmann, and Ernst Kris) and object relations theory (as found in theorists like Melanie Klein, Heinz Kohut, D. W. Winnicott), the former building more on the mechanistic ego and the latter on the "relational" self. Transformational theory, on the other hand, attempts to theorize about a religious or spiritual dimension to the human personality.

Adding specificity to these theories, ego psychological interpretations house the requisite theoretical changes to further an adaptive rendering of religion. Among the most important of the latter are reformulations of the ego (primarily the distinctions between *autoplastic vs. alloplastic adaptation* and *regression vs. regression "in the service" of the ego*) and an extension of development housed under the umbrella of life cycle theory. Concerning advances in theorizing about the ego, Freud held that the individual, because of the aggressive instinct, was always in opposition to society and its institutions. In this view, adaptation to the religious cultural superego and its regnant values required accommodation and renunciation, hence being framed by ego psychologists as an instance of "autoplastic" adaptation. "Alloplastic" adaptation, on the other hand, countered by signaling the capacity of individuals to change culture by utilizing the resources of religion. The Baptist minister and civil rights activist Marin Luther King's reliance on his faith to demand racial equality is a paradigmatic case in point, as are Martin Luther's Protestant reformulation of the overly strict, medieval, "heteronomous" Catholic understanding of morality in favor of being "justified by faith" alone and Gandhi's proclamation of *ahimsa* (nonviolence) and *satyagraha*, both taken from Indian religions, to effect social change.

The second important ego revision listed herein (that of *regression vs regression "in the service of" the ego*) stemmed from the observation that the clinical use of free association depended on a regressive process, as do the fantasied formulations of artists. Erik Erikson, in applying this concept to religious introspective techniques (like prayer), framed regression as a way of moving forward (what he called "teleological") rather than backward and fixated (which he linked with Freud and called "originological"). As we have noted, Freud emphasized that believers, faced with the existential challenges and exigencies of life, adapted by "regressing" to an earlier phase of development in which seeking the aid of the parental unit (particularly "the father") was a workable solution to one's problems. Erikson, on the other hand, framed an alternate narrative wherein one can discern in certain forms of religious introspection what he called "dim nostalgias" that, evoked through religious ideation and practices, served not simply a regressive but also a teleological function. One of these nostalgias was preoedipal, being "the simple and fervent wish for a hallucinatory sense of unity with a maternal matrix ... symbolized by the affirmative face of charity, graciously inclined, reassuring the faithful of the unconditional acceptance of those who will return to the bosom."[132] The second of these nostalgia's was oedipal, being "the paternal voice of guiding conscience, which puts an end to the simple paradise of childhood and provides a sanction for energetic action."[133] Adaptively put, such symbols at their best not only elicit developmental themes but also help repair psychological deficits. The difference between Freud and the ego psychologists on this point becomes clear when Erikson, casting doubt on Freud's myopic emphasis on the negative consequences of regression, goes on to ask,

> Must we call it regression if man thus seeks again earliest encounters of his trustful past in his efforts to reach a hoped-for and eternal future? Or do religions partake of man's ability, even as he regresses, to recover creatively? At their creative best, religions retrace our earliest inner experiences ... it is a regression which, in retracing firmly established pathways, returns to the present amplified and clarified.[134]

Ego psychological revisions of development also offered new resources for thinking about religious faith and worldviews as evolving throughout the course of the life cycle. Best represented in Erik Erikson's life cycle theory, ego psychology posited that the ego itself undergoes a process of development. In contrast to Freud, whose libido theory was confined to the development of the sexual instinct from infancy through puberty, Erikson posited eight stages of the development of the ego that ran from the preoedipal period of nursing with the mother through the challenges of old age. Each stage had both an "existential" and "ethical" dimension. For example, in the earliest, preoedipal phase of development (the stage of *infancy*) the *existential* challenge faced by the infant is whether the world is more or less a trustworthy place ("trust vs. mistrust"). The latter is decided in the main by "good-enough" mothering and the absence of serious trauma. If successfully navigated,

---

[132] E. Erikson, *Young Man Luther*, pp. 263–264. [133] Ibid. [134] Ibid.

nascent capacities for the development of the *virtue* of hope (the *capacity* to be hopeful) is facilitated. Erikson posited seven more stages of development, each with its own existential crisis and hoped-for ethical capacities: *early childhood* (autonomy vs. shame/doubt; will); *play age* (initiative vs. guilt; purpose); *school age* (industry vs. inferiority; competence); *adolescence* (identity vs. identity diffusion; fidelity); *young adulthood* (intimacy vs. isolation; love); *adulthood* (generativity vs. stagnation; care); *old age* (integrity vs. despair; wisdom). While religious ideation and practice can help one navigate the challenges of the life cycle at any stage, Erikson is particularly interested in how religion helps those with issues surrounding trust, forging an identity, exercising generativity and managing the despair of old age.

Erikson's developmental sequence was ruled by *epigenesis*, a term taken from embryology that denotes that later developmental stages unfold from previous ones (as apparent in the development of an embryo). In this hierarchical system of increasing differentiation inadequacies of early stage resolution (e.g., "being mistrustful") can be reworked and resolved in subsequent ones. For example, if one, due to a lack of preoedipal love and support, came to hold an essentially pessimistic and mistrustful view of the world, then a way to repair that deficit might be through religion. Female divinities like Mother Mary, the daily remembrance of which can be affirmed in necklaces, pins, car dashboards and scriptural referents denoting a "psychology of the face" (e.g., "The Lord make His Face to shine upon you and be gracious unto you. The Lord lift up His countenance upon you and give you peace") can repair by igniting adaptive memories of preoedipal trust and benevolence. To take another example, Erikson points to his work with adolescents, where the existential challenge was establishing a solid sense of identity (versus self-fragmentation and identity diffusion) with the corresponding capacity and virtue being that of fidelity (of "being able" to commit). A religious worldview, properly communicated, could certainly help one solidify who and what one is as well as mediate a series of ethical values and aims conducive to formulating a life cycle plan. In this sense, religion can help adolescents who are identity challenged. Erikson goes on to note how transference relationships with religious figures/pastoral psychotherapists in conjunction with the ability of religious symbols and narratives to speak to unconscious functioning and rituals that integrate one into a community, might be resources to help one revisit and resolve previously mismanaged developmental challenges. For example, in such a scenario the capacity (and virtue) linked to the preoedipal stage, that of hope, once repaired, resurrected and made existentially available, could eventually morph into a capacity more psychologically and religiously advanced, namely "faith." While only hope, and not faith proper, is available to infants, the capacity to hope is the basis for and can transmute into faith when run through religious ideation in tandem with the more advanced cognitive and volitional capacities of adolescents. In this way, then, the resources of religion can help the adolescent to form the kind of trustful relationships and solid identity for use in adapting to the vicissitudes of life.

While one can appreciate the value of advances in the theory of the ego offered by Erikson and others, a cautionary note concerning what we earlier referred to as "reflexivity" also applies here. For example, much ink has been spilt on problems concerning "stage" theories, including the specific number, linearity and "ethno" dimensions coded into what amounts to a normative developmental scheme. Indeed, Sudhir Kakar, Erikson's own student and a prominent Indian psychoanalyst and anthropologist, has sought to shear Erikson's life cycle theory of its ethno elements without jettisoning the value of ego psychological advances and his refashioning of Freud's more pejorative views on religion.[135]

Turning to object relations theory, the latter devoted its aims to the continued theorization of the "preoedipal" or narcissistic (defined in a neutral, clinical and not pejorative sense) line of development. Freud had been invested mainly in the analysis of hysteria and obsessional neuroses, a fact culture theorists attribute to his sociocultural surround and its tendency to manufacture such forms of mental distress. Only rarely did he have occasion to theorize about the "preoedipal" or "narcissistic" line of development. It was the object relations theorists who, in part due to the influx of new clinical data, undertook what became a robust round of new theorizing on the preoedipal, narcissistic line of development. That new data included the following: the preponderance of feelings of fragmentation, emptiness and meaninglessness, low self-esteem, sensitivity to disappointments, slights and failure, hypochondria, exaggerated idealization of powerful figures and the need to merge with perceived sources of strength, eruptions of archaic grandiosity, narcissistic rage and lack of empathy.[136] The data suggested looking at how Freud's second view of the ego (as described earlier in this Element), which detailed the vicissitudes of the processes of idealization, identification and internalization, might be the clue to how one's sense of self or "narcissism" was impacted through early relationships. This new line of theorizing, then, tended to downplay Freud's insistence on the biological, instinctual and triangular (i.e., oedipal) in favor of the relational and dyadic (mother–child).

---

[135] See, for example, the discussion in W.B. Parsons, *Freud and Religion* (especially chapter 7).

[136] For a good summary treatment of this see C. Lasch, *The Culture of Narcissism* (New York: W. W. Norton, 1979).

As with ego psychology one finds numerous figures (e.g., Melanie Klein, Margaret Mahler, Ronald Fairbairn) who were central to its formulation and development. Indeed, the precise details of how object relations theorists conceptualize the developmental line of narcissism vary from figure to figure. As far as the application of such theories to religious phenomena, three figures stand out: Heinz Kohut, D. W. Winnicott and Ana-Maria Rizzuto.[137] In the case of Kohut, starting from Freud's postulation of the developmental phase of primary narcissism (that phase being the origin of Romain Rolland's oceanic feeling), Kohut goes on to stipulate how that original ego feeling slowly develops into the firm, continuous stable sense of a mature "I" that he called having a "cohesive" self (i.e., the developmental line of narcissism). The infant is, of course, vulnerable, fragile and dependent on the parental unit for sustenance and support. Such vulnerability becomes heightened as the original Edenic, oceanic feeling of omnipotence and connectivity fades relative to the growing awareness of external reality, the parents as separate "objects" not under his/her control, and the demands of inner needs. In striving to counter such helplessness and vulnerability, and in the attempt to grow and achieve a measure of initiative, independence and self-cohesion, the infant's narcissistic line of development morphs into two related "archaic" narcissistic structures: the grandiose self and the idealized parent *imago*. The two structures are inexorably related yet evince different strategies the child uses to maintain self-equilibrium and adapt to a social world populated by stronger Others. The recourse to grandiosity is illustrated by developmentally phase-appropriate behaviors where, for example, the child boasts about being a god or superhero. In other words, it is normal ("phase-appropriate grandiosity") for children to inflate their feeble selves into powerful cultural figures like superheroes to create a sense of initiative and power. When faced with such behavior the parent or adult usually smiles and feeds the fantasy (i.e., "mirroring" the grandiosity of the child). So too does the parent, when the child achieves developmental milestones (riding a bicycle, tying shoes, getting good grades, etc.), spontaneously and naturally mirror and encourage the child ("good-enough" parenting). As the child matures the need for eruptions of archaic grandiosity decline due to good-enough parenting and mirroring. Archaic grandiosity is

---

[137] Additional reasons for the selection of these theorists include the fact that Kohut's transformational dimension provides a good counter to Freud's interpretation of the oceanic feeling and is hence a good marker of advances in psychoanalytic theory. Rizzuto, on the other hand, by way of noting that early object relations theorists like Klein did not comment on religion, incorporates her work as well as other early object relations theorists (e.g., M. Mahler) in addition to Freud, Kohut and Winnicott, and is thus similarly a good marker of advances in the psychoanalytic theory of religion.

gradually transformed into more mature narcissistic structures evincing acceptance of self and realistic self-esteem. If, due to trauma or poor parenting, archaic forms of expressing grandiosity are not tempered and transformed, then low self-esteem, sensitivity to slights and disappointments and outright displays of adult, archaic grandiosity may result.[138]

The second way of adapting to reality (the "idealized parental *imago*") involves the parental unit and starts with the idealization of and need to merge with them (a process Kohut refers to as merging with "self-objects"). The parents are understood by the child as centers of support and power (hence "godlike"). As development proceeds, the idealized parents slowly lose their status as moral arbiters and models for adapting to reality, being "deidealized," internalized and psychologically transformed into values, aims and blueprints for life (in short, what Kohut refers to as the building of mature "psychological structures"). If the parents are not available for idealization due to their absence or their nonempathic relation to their offspring, then the child may engage in trying to "regrow" that lost dimension of self by finding and merging with perceived "self-objects" of power. To a certain extent we all do this throughout the life cycle, but there is a difference between merging with an idealized Other that enables the morphing of archaic forms of narcissism into mature structures by mediating mature values and aims (e.g., President Kennedy's "ask not . . . "; MLK's "I have a dream") and those (e.g., totalitarian dictators) who, in demanding conformity, cater to untransformed, archaic needs to merge with a powerful, all-embracing, godlike persona. While we will resist the temptation to do so, one could certainly go on to use this model to account for the popularity of recent political figures and their social base. To conclude, if development proceeds normally, then the transformation of archaic forms of narcissistic structures to mature ones leads to realistic self-esteem, a workable set of values and the capacity to create and actualize a life plan in accordance with an accurate understanding and assessment of one's talents. If not, then a range of "narcissistic personality disorders" and their clinical signs (e.g., meaninglessness, fragmentation, hypochondria, etc.) may result. We will come back to illustrate the use of Kohut with respect to certain religious phenomena in the last section of this Element.

Another theoretical conceptualization of the developmental line of narcissism widely used to interpret religion is that offered by the British pediatrician

---

[138] For a summary statement of his psychology see H. Kohut, "Forms and Transformations of Narcissism." In P. Ornstein, ed., *The Search for the Self.* 2 vols. (New York: International Universities Press, 1978), pp. 427–460; H. Kohut and E. Wolf. "The Disorders of the Self and Their Treatment: An Outline," *International Journal of Psychoanalysis* 59 (1978), 413–425.

and psychoanalyst D. W. Winnicott. This is particularly true of his terms "transitional objects" and "transitional phenomena."[139] Based on his clinical observations of infants and children, Winnicott used such terms to explain what happens in their inner world during the developmental process of separation (from parents) and individuation (becoming a self). The critical fact was the emergence in the child's life of an object (i.e., a blanket or stuffed animal) with which the child bonds, receiving solace and nurturance. Winnicott thought that transitional objects symbolized the absent mother, the latter being inevitable during the course of a normal developmental cycle. Further, for Winnicott the initial capacity to form transitional objects is also the first attempt at symbolizing: it denotes the child's capacity to symbolize the absent parental unit. Transitional objects, in offering a remembered nurturing maternal presence, provide the self-confidence and inner calmness necessary to creatively explore, master and integrate the challenges posed by external reality as the child embarks upon the task of individuation.

Such objects punctuate the landscape of culture, art and religion. For example, one can take the little boy's relationship with the alien in the film *E.T.* (who not so coincidentally ends up hiding as part of the boy's stuffed animal collection), the tiger in the comic strip *Calvin and Hobbes* (a simple stuffed tiger when the parents are around but a living cocreator of a world of fantasy when alone with Calvin) and Linus' blanket in *Peanuts*. In such examples the transitional object points to an area of experience to which both inner psychological and outer cultural reality contribute. Hobbes, insofar as he is an object of play given to and not created by Calvin, is constituted by culture. Yet Calvin also creates Hobbes, breathing life into him and investing him with meaning in their joint efforts to playfully engage and master external reality. For Winnicott this fact points to an unchallenged "third" area of experiencing, both real and unreal, that undercuts Freud's simple opposition between inner and outer reality and their correlates, the pleasure and reality principles. This third area is what he refers to as the "substance of illusion" – an inner/outer space illumined by transitional objects. "Illusion," in this Winnicottian sense, is not so much "delusion" (as Freud would see in religious worldviews) but the more accurate and necessary psychological rendering of how human beings live their lives. In moving away from Freud's firm adherence to a strict empiricism, Winnicott offers us a new psychoanalytic epistemology for how we come to know and interact with the world.

This epistemology extends beyond the reference to transitional objects. For Winnicott, the ability to find a transitional object for use in creatively adapting

---

[139] See D. W. Winnicott, *Playing and Reality* (New York: Penguin, 1971).

to external reality designates a human capacity that expands and deepens throughout the life cycle. Examples of the latter are the investigations of science, the creative renderings of the arts and even religion. In contrast to Freud, Winnicott does not always distinguish between the three in stark terms. This lies in part due to the fact that, for Winnicott, the very definition of what constitutes a healthy person is the ability to creatively engage and master an external reality which, as an "x out there," is never fully understood or mastered. For Freud any religious worldview, because it could not be empirically confirmed, was at least an illusion, if not a form of delusion and pathology. Winnicott, on the other hand, would say that because we never get to the "x," which defines the "real" of external reality, the task of "reality acceptance" is lifelong.[140] Religion, along with science and art, offers us creative resources for engaging and adapting to the ultimately unknowable "x" that lies "out there."

Winnicott's theory has been extended to apply to one's belief system and religious worldview as a whole by the Catholic psychoanalyst Ana-Maria Rizzuto.[141] Contra Freud, Rizzuto thinks that belief "is an integral part of being human, truly human in our capacity to create nonvisible but meaningful realities capable of containing our potential for imaginative expansion beyond the boundaries of the senses."[142] Belief is always linked to a religious worldview, the latter referred to by Rizzuto as a "God-representation." It is here that Rizzuto invokes Winnicott: "God, psychologically speaking, is an illusory transitional object."[143] Indeed, it is a "special" transitional object – one formed not from "plushy fabrics" like teddy bears and blankets but from "representational materials" that, as Freud would have it, find their initial source in the primary objects of infancy and childhood. However, going further than Freud, Rizzuto argues that the God representation is an overdetermined "quilt" and "work of art" influenced by culture at large, incorporating sexual and nonsexual elements, preoedipal as well as oedipal elements, representational and well as ideational components and, in explicitly evoking Erikson's life cycle theory, capable of evolving during subsequent life stages to the extent that it can supersede developmental determinants (like oedipal dynamics and the "Father").

We can unpack the aforementioned factors that contribute to the formation of a God representation in more detail. First, culture at large is complicit. Due to the child's natural inquisitive nature and the inescapable fact of culturally available religious narratives, Rizzuto posits that a rudimentary God representation is mediated to the child through the parents and, behind them, culture at

---

[140] Ibid., chs. 1, 7.
[141] A. Rizzuto, *The Birth of the Living God* (Chicago, IL: University of Chicago Press, 1979).
[142] Ibid., p. 47.   [143] Ibid., p. 177.

large. Second, developmental factors are adduced, for a God representation becomes unavoidably imbued with relational and developmental depth. Here Rizzuto argues that the God representation can be composed of paternal and maternal elements as well as reflect preoedipal and oedipal developmental configurations. Third, what Freud refers to as "secondary process thought" also contributes to the formation of the God representation. In making clear how this happens, Rizzuto distinguishes between the "concept of God" and the "image of God." The former is the God of the theologians and philosophers fabricated at the level of secondary-process thought which follows the rules of philosophical inference, argumentation and theorizing. The "images" of God, on the other hand, find their source in the developmental vicissitudes of the representational process marked by idealization, identification and internalization. These two aspects can and do coexist in any God representation. "Image"-based religious symbols and narratives point to developmental contributions while "conceptual" aspects are due to secondary-process cognitive reflection. Finally, in adopting Erikson's notion of epigenesis, Rizzuto holds that the God representation is available for evolution, transformation and use throughout the life cycle. Epigenesis means that the God representation need not be subject to the determinism of the archaic infantile past but can be reworked, refined and transformed. Crucial to the latter process is the ongoing integration of the conceptual aspects of the God representation with the deeper developmentally and interpersonally based images of God. A dialectical process between the two is posited as taking place through significant experiences, idealized mentor figures of all kinds (from a psychoanalyst to a pastor) who elicit transference, and the individual psychical work of self-scrutiny and self-reflection. Through such auspices a process akin to the analytic session takes place, resulting in the integration and transformation of conceptual and image-based aspects of the God representation. In this schema, "conversion" is defined as the "ego-syntonic release from repression in a given individual of an earlier (or even present) parental representation linked to a God representation."[144] Importantly, Rizzuto thinks that a God representation, being a quilt and work of art to which multiple sources contribute, can contain transformational mystical insights as well: "The developmental process of forming a God representation is exceedingly complex and is influenced by a multitude of cultural, social, familiar, individual phenomena ranging from the deepest biological levels of human experience to the subtlest of spiritual realizations."[145]

---

[144] Ibid., p. 51.

[145] Ibid., p. 182. One can also note that the use of Rizzuto's theory, like that of Freud, Erikson and others, must be linked to reflexivity. Most notably, her theory has a Western bias, which leads

This latter point is a segue to the attempt within psychoanalysis to offer space for a generic religious or spiritual dimension to the unconscious. Such "transformational" models can be found as early as Erik Erikson. For example, in addition to the two "nostalgias" (preoedipal and oedipal) cited earlier, Erikson noted that monastic techniques enabled access to an even deeper "third nostalgia," which references "the pure self itself, the unborn core of creation, the – as it were, preparental – center where God is pure nothing: *ein lauter Nichts*, in the words of Angelus Silesius." Erikson goes on to note how

> God is so designated in many ways in Eastern mysticism … one way of liberating man from his existential delimitations, is to retrace the steps of the development of the I, to forego even object relations in the most primitive sense, to step down and back to the borderline where the I emerged from its matrix … the Eastern form cultivates the art of deliberate self-loss: Zen Buddhism is probably its most systematic form.[146]

An alternate formulation can be found in another transformational theorist, the British psychoanalyst Wilfred Bion. While Bion's thought is complex, what is of interest to us is a specific concept that reflects a transformational dimension, that of "O", which he defined as "ultimate reality, absolute truth, the godhead, the infinite, the thing-in-itself. O does not fall in the domain of knowledge or learning save incidentally; it can be 'become,' but it cannot be known."[147] Bion insisted that O is unknowable, ineffable (beyond language), a "groundless ground," and, as a result, it cannot be fully apprehended by human cognition. Since he was influenced by Kant, one could say that the closest philosophical correlate would be Kant's concept of the *noumenon* (or "thing-in-itself"). With respect to Western religious thought he is closest to "apophatic" (unsaying) theology, a strong line of mystical thought found in numerous figures from Dionysius to St. John of the Cross (who Bion cited numerous times in this regard). At the same time, O is seen by Bion as the foundational ground of psychoanalysis and of psychoanalytic therapy. In the contemporary scene, the integration of a groundless ground with psychoanalytic therapy has made his formulations particularly attractive to psychoanalysts who are also Buddhist meditation teachers. They find in Bion a theoretical bridge allowing a connection between the "nondual" ground accessed through meditation with psychoanalytic theorizing about developmental contributions.[148]

---

one to ask: how could the notion of a God representation be used in a Theravada Buddhist culture? See the discussion in W.B. Parsons, *Freud and Religion*, ch. 7.

[146] E. Erikson, *Young Man Luther*, pp. 264, 119.

[147] P. Cooper, *Zen Insight, Psychoanalytic Action* (New York: Routledge, 2019), pp. 98–99.

[148] Ibid.

A third transformational theorist is the French psychoanalyst Jacques Lacan. Like Bion, Lacan's formulations are complex.[149] What interests us here are his concepts of the "Real" and "jousissance." From a religious perspective the Real is akin to a "thing-in-itself," an Absolute that is ineffable, undifferentiated, and primordial. Importantly Lacan, in referencing a philosophical version of this primordial Reality, pointed to the Neoplatonic sage Plotinus and his rendering, in his famous book *The Enneads*, of what he called the "One." In further speaking of the Plotinian "One," Lacan states that it is linked to a form of desire or Eros he called *jouissance*. The latter is a special form of desire that "goes beyond" sexual objects. Lacan found such a *jouissance* in Christian mystics like St. Teresa and her bridal mysticism. The latter is charged with sexual metaphors yet, in Lacan's view, is also charged with an energy, both pleasurable and painful, that "goes beyond" sexuality. A portrait of *jouissance* in the religious register is seen in Bernini's statue of "Teresa in Ecstasy," which depicts Teresa lying prone while an angel pierces her lower abdomen with his spear. Commenting on the Freudian take on this statue Lacan says: "she's coming, there is no doubt about it." He then adds: "And what is her *jouissance*, her coming from?"[150] His answer is that Teresa's mystical-erotic utterances "go beyond" developmental considerations, thus they are directed to a deeper form of Eros. In asking us to open up psychoanalytic metapsychology to a conception of mystical desire, Lacan stated that mystical utterances were the "best thing you can read," adding that his own work should be regarded as essentially "of the same order" as mysticism.[151] As some have observed, Lacan has shifted psychoanalytic conceptions of language, the unconscious, truth and healing toward a perspective commensurate with philosophical and religious mysticism.[152]

A transformational dimension is also evident in Heinz Kohut's concept of "cosmic narcissism." The latter is framed as a developmentally mature attainment indicative of ethical and existential achievement above and beyond the results of even a successful analysis. Kohut insists that cosmic narcissism is statelike, consisting in "a shift of the narcissistic cathexis from the self to

---

[149] As with Freud, Erikson and Rizzuto, one can spy the need for reflexivity (as J. Kristeva and others have shown) with respect to the phallocentric architecture of Lacan's theory. Indeed, Kakar's appropriation of the transformational component of Lacan's theory as undertaken later in this Element shows such reflexivity at work. A good example of a feminist inspired use of transformational theory that utilizes the formulations of L. Irigaray can be found in E. Wolfson, *Through a Speculum That Shines* (Princeton, NJ: Princeton University Press, 1997).

[150] J. Lacan, "God and the Jouissance of Women." In J. Mitchell and J. Rose, eds., *Feminine Sexuality: Jacques Lacan and the Ecole Freudian* (New York: W. W. Norton, 1982), p. 147.

[151] Ibid.

[152] See R. Webb and M. Sells, "Lacan and Bion: Psychoanalysis and the Mystical Language of Unsaying." *Theory and Psychology* 5(2) (1995), 195–215.

a concept of participation in a supraindividual and timeless existence."[153] Cosmic narcissism "transcends the bounds of the individual" and one lives "sub specie aeternitas" without elation or anxiety, bathed in a continual communion with a contentless, supraordinate Self, participating in "supraindividual ideals and the world with which one identifies."[154] Importantly, Kohut goes on to conjoin to his religio-ethical ideal a cultural agenda. In his essay "On Leadership" Kohut goes so far as to suggest the need for a new, unchurched rational religion, "an as yet uncreated system of mystical rationality which could take the place of the religions of the past."[155] He points to "instances of heroic men of constructive political action who have achieved a transformation of their narcissism into a contentless, inspiring personal religion," further opining that humanity will have to produce such types in greater numbers in order to survive.[156] As to who might embody such an achievement, Kohut points to Dag Hammarskjöld, the former secretary-general of the United Nations: "Dag Hammarskjöld ... an example of this type, describes his contentless mysticism in the following words: 'Faith is a state of mind and of the soul ... the language of religion is (only) a set of formulas which register a basic religious experience.'"[157]

3 Toward a Revised Psychoanalytic Theory of Religion

The foregoing has detailed Freud's views on monotheism and the history of the subsequent multidisciplinary critiques of his position. We further indicated that Freud's classic psychoanalytic formulations must abide by certain cautionary tales. To reaffirm the nomenclature linked to the latter, there is the need for *reflexivity* (i.e., being mindful of its potential ethnopsychological dimensions and the reproduction of patriarchy, racism and colonialism), *dialogue* (with social sciences, humanistic disciplines and religious intellectuals), and *inclusivity* (not simply classic psychoanalytic formulations but ego-psychological, object-relational and transformational).

Even so, the variety of religious phenomena is such that one cannot exclude an unqualified use of classical oedipal theory. In certain cases the latter may well be the preferred psychoanalytic model. In other cases one might do better to turn to later advances in psychoanalytic theory in conjunction with reflexivity and dialogue. In other words, it behooves one to be well-enough informed about not only the history of the development of psychoanalytic models but also the need for reflexivity and dialogue to know which available psychoanalytic tools to use

---

[153] H. Kohut, "Forms and Transformations of Narcissism," pp. 455–456.　　[154] Ibid.

[155] H. Kohut, "On Leadership." In C. Strozier, ed., *Self Psychology and the Humanities* (New York: W. W. Norton, 1985), p. 70.

[156] Ibid.　　[157] Ibid.

in selected instances. To facilitate the art of application we will, in the following, offer some portable lessons drawn from the application of not only Freud but also a broad range of psychoanalytic models in tandem with our suggested revisions. To be sure, the illustrations we will adduce constitute but a sampling of how the variety of psychoanalytic tools might be applied. In no way is it assumed that the specific strategies they exhibit are necessarily to be followed to the letter. The strategies employed are tailored to the specific examples analyzed and are both flexible and falsifiable with respect to alternate cases. The basic value of our applications, then, resides in the fact that they model a general direction going forward.

3.1 Freud and Peter Parker

We can start by pointing to a simple example of how an unqualified use of classical oedipal theory has its merits, and do so by turning to the most popular figure in the Marvel Universe: Spiderman. Psychoanalytically speaking, the "origin story" of Spidey is a paradigmatic instance of oedipal conflict. That story features an adolescent boy (Peter Parker), often bullied and shunned for his nerdiness, who is bitten by a radioactive spider. While oblivious of this fact, he later finds that he has real powers: super strength, wallcrawling, a tingling spider sense and the ability to produce a sticky, weblike substance. It is not far-fetched to see the connection between the latter and the additional muscle mass, height, growth and ability to produce a sticky substance associated with male pubescence. This is confirmed in a recent installment of the movie series featuring Spiderman when Peter, upon receiving a new suit, says, "it's a bit tight in the old web-shooters." More to the point, in this fantasy Oedipus plays the featured role. Peter Parker becomes Spiderman on that fateful day when he intentionally lets a robber escape only to find that the robber went on to kill his father substitute (Uncle Ben). Devastated with sorrow, regret and guilt (feelings that indicate an unconscious identification with the robber's act and hence patricidal urges), Peter (at the behest of his superego) vows to spend his life fighting crime, complete with a new persona, costume and, above all, the need to keep his "real identity" secret. The latter, now read as pointing to oedipal crime and guilt, becomes the determining factor that constantly interferes in his relationships with women: Aunt May, Betty Brandt, Mary Jane Watson and Gwen Stacey. Indeed, psychoanalysts would say that this particular cultural production is ruled by an oedipal gradient. The creators of Spiderman (Stan Lee, Jack Kirby, Steve Ditko) found a way to portray the plight of male adolescence imaginatively enough to elicit the allegiance of male unconscious contents in an experience-distant manner. By identifying with Spidey we literally act out an oedipal crisis and its resolution, even if momentarily.

Drawing on our stated need for *inclusivity* within the psychoanalytic theory of religion, we can add that there is a significant difference between the oedipal and the later, object relations analysis of Spiderman. In the latter the emphasis of the origin myth is not Peter Parker's feeling of guilt over letting a robber kill Uncle Ben but the fact that he became Spiderman as a result of being "infected" by a poisonous, radioactive spider. In the psychoanalytic view spiders are symbols of the venomous, suffocating, castrating mother. To be bitten and infected by one is a metaphor for a developmental sequence in which one never received maternal mirroring and empathy. The results are feelings of inadequacy, low self-esteem and exhibitionistic outbursts of grandiosity (namely, thinking one is a superhero). This fits with the framing of Peter Parker as a nerdish, unpopular, weak high school teenager beset by bullies. The idea here is that we all, to a certain extent, have a need to "be grandiose." By identifying with Spiderman, we enact that grandiosity to varying degrees to appease our need for greatness and mirroring. One could say the same for any of the "heroes" that populate the Marvel Universe. We pick and choose between them in the service of our varying psychological needs. Of course, it is one thing to have cultural outlets like the Marvel Universe to appease one's need (through identification) for grandiosity and mirroring but an entirely different one to offer religious narratives that authorize individuals to proclaim that they are the second coming of a messiah. The underlying psychology is the same, even if the institutions (art; religion) offer different solutions, some of them dangerous, for those who are narcissistically challenged. It is one of the psychoanalytic contributions to culture that we have a method to distinguish between such alternatives.

3.2 The *Unbehagen* of Religion, Gender and Sexuality

Turning to specifically religious phenomena, we indicated in the first section of this Element that Freud's cultural works were designed in part to target the "ontological" status of religion by focusing his critique on what he called the cultural superego and its unpsychological proceedings. By way of commenting further, it is initially helpful to distinguish between art and religion. Art, by which Freud meant literature, theater and visual media such as photography, painting and sculpture, and which we can modernize to include films, television and social media, serves the aims of civilization by authorizing the free play of fantasy activity. For Freud the unconscious driver of all of the latter examples are unrequited sexual and aggressive wishes and the need for identity and

affirmation. In this sense, the cultural function of art, through individual participation, is to fulfill such fantasies and deficits.

Those wedded to religious belief systems would counter by saying that
secular examples like Spiderman are instances of the human imagination at
work and not the directives of a holy and sacred monotheistic source. Societies
have historically framed the epistemological status of religion and its institutional accouterments as proceeding not from humans but from a divine ground.
For Freud, it is that very framing that serves to actualize religion's specific
psychological function and dynamics vis-à-vis the individual. Those functions
include fostering acts of repression, feelings of guilt and fear, tribalism, racism
and the stunting of the intellect. As a result, and contrary to art, expressions of
the religious imagination are not seen by Freud as occasions for introspection,
edification and individuation but function to repress its free play. This is the
heart of the problem. For Freud there is no "ontos" to which the religious
imagination is directed. The latter is a (mistaken) reification of culture, and
the job of psychoanalysis is to translate religious expressions back into its true
source, which, like art, is the human imagination.

Turning now to Freud's targeting of the content of the cultural superego, one
of the ways in which religious institutions are unpsychological and exacerbate
unbehagen concerns sexuality. As we saw earlier, and as argued in his *Totem
and Taboo*, Freud was convinced that sexuality, channeled and expressed
through the vicissitudes marked by the dynamics of Oedipus, was at the root
of the civilization, religion and morality. From its beginnings, then, religion and
the cultural superego aimed at monitoring and regulating sexuality. Indeed,
recall that one of the very first laws (the taboo of exogamy) of civilization aimed
at forbidding the most fervent sexual wish of the unconscious, namely, incest
(a law that, while in the service of Eros by enabling the "greater unity" outside
the family, Freud also referred to as "perhaps the most drastic mutilation which
man's erotic life has in all time experienced").[158] Of course, with the development of civilization, the restrictions of sexual life became much more wide
ranging. At times Freud speaks highly of such efforts of civilization, for
example, how aim-inhibited love, paradigmatically manifested in the bonds of
friendship, helped create and sustain ever greater unities of peoples. But what
about religious proclamations concerning genital sexuality? Freud was well
aware that the Judeo-Christian tradition valorized the unchanging, divinely
inspired norm of heterosexual monogamy. This was not necessarily a problem
for it jibed well with the majority of those heterosexually inclined as well as
with Freud's adherence to the Darwinian propagation of the species. On the

---

[158] Freud, *Civilization and Its Discontents*, S.E., vol. 21, p. 104.

other hand, like many aspects of the cultural superego, it was unpsychological in that it did not take into account the diversity of individual sexual impulses. The data Freud gathered through his patients and self-analysis revealed that the sexual impulses and aims of human beings did not always fit under the normative banner of heterosexual monogamy. And so it is that Freud said that the requirement "that there shall be a single kind of sexual life for everyone, disregards the dissimilarities, whether innate or acquired, in the sexual constitution of human beings; it cuts off a fair number of them from sexual enjoyment, and so becomes the course of serious injustice."[159] In this regard Freud, when asked by a mother to "cure" her gay son, responded that homosexuality was "nothing to be ashamed of, no vice, no degradation"; that "it cannot be classified as an illness"; and that it was "a great injustice to persecute homosexuality as a crime – and a cruelty, too."[160] Freud's solution was predictably consistent: the cultural superego must be changed in ways that accord with the actual psychological constitution of individuals – a fact that has come to pass in no small measure due to the social authority of a clinical space (i.e., psychoanalysis) that has authorized the expression of alternate ways of expressing and fulfilling one's sexual needs.

What is more problematic is when the religious intolerance of anything outside of heterosexual monogamy is enforced. In illustrating a contemporary instance of the latter recall how, in the first section of this Element, we called attention to the fact that Freud lent a qualified approval to religious forms of psychotherapy. In now coming back to that qualified stance, we can add he cautioned that they, as opposed to psychoanalysis, could not effect a permanent cure. The reason, he says, is that they conceal the play of unconscious forces. In other words, they cannot eventuate in the more lasting "education" of the unconscious and its instincts. While religious forms of therapy may well lead to a happier life that is adaptive, it does so on the basis of offering illusions that signify the continued presence and influence of infantilism. In so doing, they leave themselves open to the charge of enabling the "return of the repressed." Moreover, the possibility remains that religious forms of therapeutic intervention might, in pushing a specific value-laden, "suggestive" worldview, fail to empathically connect with the uniqueness and deepest core of the individual, preferring to enforce a form of "higher" religious repression. A contemporary example of the latter lies in those religious counseling services devoted to "curing" members of the LGBT community. The kind of violence and *unbehagen* Freud abhorred is, in fact, represented by just such "therapies."

---

[159] Ibid.   [160] "A Letter from Freud." *American Journal of Psychiatry*, 1951, 786–787.

Going further, and bringing in examples of some of our suggested revisions, there are other instances of gender identity and sexuality in the theistic tradition that are better addressed by the revisions of *reflexivity* and *inclusiveness* – revisions that also engage the psychoanalytic dialogue with Eastern religions (the *psychology–comparativist dialogue*). In this regard we can turn to the Indian psychoanalyst Sudhir Kakar and his reflections on the Hindu tantric actualization of the aim of divine androgyny. For Kakar, as for Freud, there should be no one normative template for how the cultural superego monitors gender identity and sexuality. People are different, and a certain flexibility in the religo-cultural superego needs to reflect that diversity.

Kakar's initial move is to show how this is the case with respect to one such tantric practitioner, that of Sri Ramakrishna, and his quest to actualize the divine within. This means a thorough engagement with the religio-cultural context that guided Ramakrishna's sense of self, sexuality and gender identity. In the case of Ramakrishna's desire to achieve liberation, Kakar thinks that the tantric striving for deeper insight into the foundational nature of the self cannot be reduced to pathology or regressive states. On one hand, he understands that what he calls the "motivational skein" of the religious intent to seek the divine is complex and may be overdetermined in a way that includes developmental contributions. On the other, he departs from Freud when he includes one of the "transformational" theorists, Jacques Lacan (who he refers to as one of the "mystics of psycho-analysis"), to legitimate the psycho-mystical quest for the divine:

> Lacan . . . has postulated that man's psychic life constantly seeks to deal with a primordial state of affairs which he calls the Real. The Real itself is unknowable, though we constantly create myths as its markers. Perhaps the principal myth involves the rupture of a basic union, the separation from the mother's body, leaving us with a fundamental feeling of incompletion. The fantasies around this insufficiency are universal, governing the psyche of both patients and analysts alike. In the psyche, this lack is translated as desire, and the human venture is a history of desire as it ceaselessly loses and discovers itself in (what Lacan calls) The Imaginary and, with the advent of language, The Symbolic order. Born of rupture, desire's fate is an endless quest for the lost object; all real objects merely interrupt the search . . . The mystical quest seeks to rescue from primal repression the constantly lived contrast between an original interlocking and a radical rupture. The mystic, unlike most others, does not mistake his hunger for its fulfillment. If we are all fundamentally perverse in the play of our desire, then the mystic is the only one who seeks to go beyond the illusion of The Imaginary and, yes, also the *maya* of The Symbolic register.[161]

---

[161] S. Kakar, *The Analyst and the Mystic* (Chicago, IL: University of Chicago Press. 1991), p. 27.

The Hindu tantric aim of achieving the Real is linked to a new framing of gender identity: that of divine androgyny. In Kakar's hands, such an ideal is not seen as abnormal or anything other than one of many equal, if different, cultural and religious solutions to the existential challenges surrounding universal conflicts about gender identity and sexual orientation. To this end, he notes that object relations theory does not posit, as did Freud, that both boys and girls are initially born as "little men" but, because the mother is the first "object" with which we identity, as "little women." For males, this means that the de-repression and "ego-syntonic" (i.e., accepted by the ego) integration of one's primary femininity is a developmental task – one recognized in Hinduism and targeted by many of its tantric practices.[162] Armed with this new model, Kakar interprets Ramakrishna's various practices activating what some object relations theorists call the "pure female element."[163] The de-repression and integration of the latter may well be heralded, in certain cultures and religions (as with tantra), as a gender ideal (i.e., divine androgyny) to be realized.

Kakar then links the achievement of divine androgyny to a specific form of the multiple, available and relatively equal modes of adaptation to reality. One such Western ideal mode valorizes the need for continual "doing," "mastery" and even "active opposition." Tantra, however, valorizes an alternate mode, as is reflected in the Hindu notions of *ananda* and "focused receptivity." The latter terms are defined with respect to a permanent form of psychological transformation centered around a receptive, empathic attunement with the flow of everyday events, championing a subjectivity imbued with the delight of creative apperception and the virtues of simply "being" and the more relaxed attitude of "reception absorption."[164] In other words, by offering a transformational, reflexive portrait of gender and sexuality, Kakar shows a way out of the hegemony of an unreflexive essentialist view that can prejudice psychoanalytic interpretations of religious phenomena, particularly those found in non-Western religio-cultural systems.

3.3 The *Unbehagen* of Religious Doctrines

We have seen that Freud endeavored to show the value of the view that a "developmental infrastructure" exists to religious commands and ideologies (which is to say to the cultural superego). The case in point we summarized was

---

[162] See S. Kakar, *Shamans, Mystics, Doctors*, ch. 6 ("Tantra and Tantric Healing").

[163] S. Kakar, *The Analyst and the Mystic*, ch. 1.

[164] Ibid., p. 34; S. Kakar, "Tantra and Tantric Healing," pp. 155–179.

that of his critique of the love command. In now extending that discussion, Freud's analysis is relevant for the contemporary scene insofar as he links the love command to what he calls the "narcissism of minor differences." In unpacking this linkage Freud notes that in asking us to "love universally" the love command fails to take into account the displaced aggression such an unrealizable command invariably occasions. It is always possible says Freud, to bind a certain number of people into a group through love. But this also leads to a form of tribalism in which other groups of people, namely the "out" group, are left over to receive the various expressions of their aggressiveness. Freud notes that when St. Paul "posited universal love between men as the foundation of his Christian community, extreme intolerance on the part of Christendom towards those who remained outside it became the inevitable consequence."[165] Indeed, he wryly notes that "the Jewish people, scattered everywhere, have rendered the most useful services to the civilizations of the countries that have been their hosts."[166] Along these lines, continues Freud, it is hardly an accident that "the dream of a Germanic world-dominion called for antisemitism as its complement."[167]

The psychological dynamic of the "narcissism of minor differences" is portable, applying to everything from the ongoing strife between Catholics and Protestants (notably in Great Britain and Ireland in the later part of the twentieth century) and the Sunni and Shia (e.g., in Iran and Saudi Arabia) to early twenty-first-century American anti-immigration sentiment. Significantly, one could extend this portable lesson to apply to cousin theological doctrines, most dramatically that of predestination and the various formulations concerning the end time. While not all religious denominations valorize the doctrine of predestination, the Weberian framing of a "Protestant work ethic" is quite familiar, having become part of our Western cultural superego. Yet the framing of God as wholly transcendent and beyond the reach of human supplication – which then forces one (through hard work) to create the illusion of "being chosen" – is but one interpretation of scripture. Freud would explain its popularity as reflecting the general tenor of the relationship between fathers and sons in Calvin's era, now available writ large in a specific framing of a religious doctrine about the nature of God and his relationship to the believer. For many, predestination is attractive not only because it caters to the framing of a distant "Father God" who needs to be constantly pleased but also because it is a theological rationalization of tribalism, of "being chosen," hence catering to narcissistic needs for love, mirroring and acceptance. The latter, in turn, is susceptible to forms of tribal violence, of which the doctrine of an apocalyptic

---

[165] Freud, *Civilization and Its Discontents*, S.E., vol. 21, p. 114.   [166] Ibid.   [167] Ibid., p. 115.

divine judgment (the "end times") is an extreme form. What is pathological is that such doctrines are nothing more than imaginative creations, rationalized fantasies as it were, of developmental themes, needs and conflicts. The frightful next step is when they are co-opted by religion and used to justify social actions, an analysis worth considering given their contemporary status as doctrinal mainstays in religious traditions as seemingly opposite as those of radical terrorists (e.g., Isis) and certain Christian members of American political parties, both "tribes" of which continue to impact contemporary world politics. The danger is that we fail to see how we collectively create and sustain such doctrines (through developmentally determined imaginative activity), rationalizing and "ontologizing" them through religious institutions and the cultural superego, then using them as justifications to enact violence. In warning of the primitivity of the human species, Freud was signifying the ways in which institutional religion was complicit in helping developmental factors (i.e., pathological narcissism, oedipal distress) win out over reason and the survival of the species (which is to say, religion "in the service of" Thanatos).

3.4 The Rise of the Megachurch

Expanding on these concepts, the application of psychoanalysis to another contemporary institution, that of the megachurch, allows us to continue to see the value of dialogue with respect to the other social sciences. As a prelude to our analysis, we can point out that social scientists, by way of adopting a sociology of knowledge approach to the shifting data sets and subsequent need to falsify psychoanalytic metapsychology, have observed that Freud's data set was fueled by an emerging industrial society where Oedipus, obsessional neurosis and hysteria were exacerbated by the then extant economic and familial organizations as well as by a hegemonic patriarchy complete with essentialized social constructions of gender. Oedipus, as mentioned earlier, may be a universal possibility but, contra Freud and his *Totem and Taboo*, not necessarily a universal actuality. Similarly, that same group of theorists will point out that, put colloquially, ego psychology is what you get when you take classical psychoanalysis out of Vienna and ship it on a boat to New York City with its capitalistic valorization of an executive ego. Again, object relations theorizing is bound to happen when, in the aftermath of World War Two, one finds many families without fathers, mothers who must work and latchkey children (the latter all too bereft of parental monitoring and mirroring) while transformational theory is in part fueled by the growing presence of that ideal type Max Weber referred to as the "inner-worldly mystic." There is, then, a fit between cultural soil, clinical data sets, and the inevitable falsification of theory.

In the case of the rising popularity of the megachurch, a sociologically informed use of *inclusive* psychoanalysis has much to offer. For example, in the analysis of the largest megachurch in the United States (Joel Osteen's Lakewood Church) offered by Christine Miller and Nathan Carlin, they begin by affirming those psychosocial analyses (notably Christopher Lasch's work *The Culture of Narcissism*) that point to how the disruption of the nuclear family, in tandem with shifts in economic conditions and the sociopolitical sphere, exacerbated the prevalence of narcissistic disorders in the clinic. In modeling civilization as a kind of "organism," the cultural imagination responded by not only occasioning the falsification of psychoanalytic theory but, additionally, authorizing the rise of other healing venues, such as the megachurch, in which self-disorders could be addressed in an experience-distant, adaptive fashion. As such, and fittingly, Miller and Carlin center their analysis around Heinz Kohut's mapping of the trajectory of the narcissistic (object-relational) line of development. Osteen and his fellow pastors, they argue, are best thought of in terms of eliciting and then addressing idealizing transferences. In so doing, they mimic the psychological gradient found in the emergence of another religious figure, the guru, who also came to cultural awareness and popularity in part due to the same socioeconomic conditions. To briefly unpack that argument, it was during the cultural tumult of the 1950s and 1960s that narcissistic self-deficits emerged in the clinic. The popularity of the figure of the guru, then, was in part due to the collective need for cultural self-objects ripe for idealization. For those with narcissistic deficits the guru, framed as "perfect" (enlightened) and promising salvation, was attractive in that it engaged narcissistic themes and afforded the opportunity for a "developmental second chance."[168] Miller and Carlin think that such an analysis is portable and extends to Osteen and his fellow pastors (gurus) at Lakewood. The variety of pastor-guru figures, aside from Osteen, found at Lakewood ensured that one's choice would be directed by "parental style," meaning the extent to which the pastor-guru exhibits characteristics reminiscent of one's actual parents. The relation to the pastor-guru is characterized as marked by submission, devotion and idealization. The latter, in turn, necessarily facilitates regression. Once in this relationship, then, the power of the pastor-guru to heal is enhanced. An "idealizing transference" is induced where every move, glance, touch and word of the guru becomes an opportunity for the seeker to feel valued, mirrored and loved. Such a transference could result in an adaptive, healing relationship insofar as the reconstitution of the developmental

---

[168] See S. Kakar, "The Guru As Healer," in Kakar, *The Analyst and the Mystic*, pp. 35–54.

process of idealization and internalization helps one transform archaic narcis-sistic structures into mature ones.

Lakewood, then, is framed as facilitating, in an experience-distant manner, an adaptive, healing encounter. Miller and Carlin go on to list the multiple ways it serves to elicit idealizing transferences and opportunities for healing narcissistic self-deficits. The latter include: (1) a "light" theology that empha-sizes a nonjudgmental attitude and the value of collective solidarity; (2) sermons that mediate total acceptance, mirroring of grandiosity and affirmation ("You are God's masterpiece … God accepts you … God approves of you"); (3) the presence of therapeutic handlers during the service who are available to listen to the suffering and complaints of parishioners.[169] In effect, what we have here is another form of suggestive-supportive ther-apy. Lakewood "cures" in an experience-distant way by offering religious narratives and transference figures that elicit unconscious content while assuaging narcissistic deficits. That said, it should be added as a cautionary tale that a more sinister series of events may ensue, as is evinced in the guru scandal literature. If the guru or pastor is suffering from unresolved narcis-sistic issues of their own (e.g., the archaic grandiose need to be admired as a god) while the seeker suffers from low esteem, then abuse can result. In the scandal literature this can range from sexual abuse to inappropriate financial demands to actual violence.

3.5 The Case of QAnon

The cultural ascendancy of another sociopolitical ideology, that of QAnon, affords us the opportunity to see how another dialogical project, that of psychoanalysis in dialogue with theology, can offer an edifying series of analyses.

To begin, we need a basic delineation of the topic. The central narrative at the heart of QAnon is that the US government is filled with Satanists and pedophiles who, among other things, sacrifice children and drink their blood. QAnon, then, is but a revised iteration of its previous incarnation as Satanic ritual abuse (SRA). The basic template of the latter, like QAnon, is the existence of an international underground network of the elite and wealthy who are Satanists, their core ritual being the abuse (including the blood sacrifice) of children. The SRA was "found out" through the discovery of trauma expressed in clinical sessions. The trauma was initially linked by

---

[169] C. Miller and N. Carlin, "Joel Osteen As Cultural Self-Object: Meeting the Needs of the Group Self and Its Individual Members in and from the Largest Church in America." *Pastoral Psychology* 59, 2010, 27–51.

multiple psychologists (e.g., Bennet Braun, Richard Kluft) to the prevalence of dissociative phenomena and multiple personality disorder. This led to the creation of investigative bodies (e.g., ISSMP&D; S.M.A.R.T.) and invariably to the cultural spread of the reality of the SRA through the gullibility of famous figures (e.g., Gloria Steinem, Geraldo Rivera, Oprah Winfrey), famous cases (e.g., the Ingram case) and social media. The question is whether such a global network of Satanists in fact exists. The psychoanalytic scholar Benjamin Beit-Hallahmi undermines the reality of the SRA through studies critiquing the reliability of clinically accessed "recovered memories," adding to the latter the skeptical conclusions of judicial interventions (e.g., US vs. Judith Peterson; FBI investigations), the dubious motives of those involved, and plain common sense (such a religion could not have existed unknown for decades). In so doing, Beit-Hallahmi takes to task the complicity of many of the aforementioned mental health professionals and celebrities as well as the gullibility of the believing public. To be sure, Beit-Hallahmi is not saying that child abuse and incest do not occur. Rather, he shows how the notion of a transgenerational, underground Satanic religion involving millions is a fiction. The problem is that this specific conspiracy theory is kept alive and believed by a wide swath of the population.[170]

Granting this, then, there are resources within the psychoanalytic toolkit and its dialogical projects to unpack and critique the way in which QAnon engages and then keeps ahold of the believer. For example, while QAnon is understood in some religious communities as an adjunct to monotheistic religions like Christianity, in reality it promotes dualism (a portable fact that applies to many adherents of the three great monotheisms). Those in the fold constantly parrot the age-old battle between God and Satan, good and evil as authorized by the echoes of the religio-cultural superego. The defense mechanism of splitting, which is manifested at the metaphysical level (i.e., God and Satan), has its counterpart at the psychological level, where the splitting becomes a useful means to repress unconscious content. It is here that a portable lesson, drawn from the dialogue with theology, is revealing. Specifically, one can turn to the evolution of belief found in St. Augustine's *Confessions*.[171] The inner world of the QAnon adherent is not unlike the adolescent Augustine who, as he later came to see, used the Manichean dualistic worldview to defend against sexual and aggressive instinctual

---

[170] B. Beit-Hallahmi, *Flesh and Blood: Interrogating Freud on Human Sacrifice, Real and Imagined* (Leiden: Brill, 2019).

[171] For a history of the engagement within the psychology–theology dialogue as well as a specific take on it, see W. B. Parsons, *Freud and Augustine in Dialogue* (Charlottesville: University of Virginia Press, 2013).

demands of his unconscious. As Augustine retrospectively put it, the notion of the existence of an "evil" coeternal ontological substance ("a Dyad – anger as in deeds of violence, and lust as in sins of impurity"[172]) allowed him to forestall the need for introspection and the reformation of the *imago dei* within. Of course to the modern mind Augustine's reflections about the Dyad are thoroughly Freudian. Indeed, for Freud the devil (in this case the Dyad), culturally constituted through psychic splitting, is but the projected personification of repressed, unwanted unconscious instincts.[173] In the case of QAnon what invariably happens is that the splitting of the psyche and repression of unconscious contents engages another defense mechanism, that of projection, which serves to dress those very contents onto the "other," in this case being the out-group (e.g., people of color, women, another political party or another religion). What we have in the QAnon adherent, then, is not an accurate depiction of "the other" but, using Augustine's own terminology, an accurate depiction, albeit in disguised and projected form, of the state of their own "disordered" personality, now defended against through the ego mechanisms of splitting and projection. Unlike Augustine, who abandoned Manicheanism and moved to a Christianized Neoplatonism (evil as "privation"), such believers seem incapable of moving beyond the psychological cage wrought by dualistic modes of thought. From a theological perspective, then, they are making God "in their own image" and the dualism they espouse is but a mirror reflecting the contents of their inner world. Turning to object relations theory, the attendant tribalism created with fellow believers serves to shore up their need for identity while buttressing deficits in the narcissistic sector of their personality. What psychoanalysis gifts those imprisoned in such psychological primitivity is freedom, should they rise to the occasion. Unfortunately, the infantile response is not introspection and the reformation of the *imago dei* within but doubling down through repression and then "acting out" through the exercise of violence – a choice that has been repeated time and again throughout history. It is in this light we should interpret Freud's pessimistic response to Lou Andreas-Salome that, as instances of this sort seem to multiply despite the introspective tools advanced by science and certain forms of religion, mankind was "organically unfitted" for civilization: "We have to abdicate, and the Great Unknown ... will sometime repeat such an experiment with another race."[174] It is the continued primitivity of the human psyche and its promotion by those so possessed in positions of religio-cultural power that is contributing to the self-inflicted demise of humanity.

---

[172] See Augustine's *Confessions*, 4.5.   [173] See A. Rizzuto, *Birth of the Living God*, pp. 20ff.

[174] E. Jones, *The Life and Work of Sigmund Freud*. 3 vols. (New York: Basic Books, 1957), p. 177.

3.6 Concluding Reflections

To reiterate, this Element is but a sampling of the uses of psychoanalytic methodology to analyze religion, monotheism and its various linked doctrines, commands and accouterments. Taking them, then, as portable lessons, we can sum up by saying that when applying Freud and his psychoanalytic heirs on religion it is useful to keep in mind their collective intent. Psychoanalysis is not only that therapeutic intervention that contributes to lessening the "unease" in individuals through active therapy but also, through the analysis of cultural pathology, the unease created by social institutions. In other words, psycho-analysis is not only offering means to transform individuals but also the tools for advancing social-structural change. Transformed individuals, guided by the psychoanalytic command *Wo Es war, soll Ich warden* ("where Id was, there Ego shall be"), would necessarily be enjoined to do the further work of transforming the institutional structures that rule the discontents of culture. As stated earlier, Freud remarked to the Protestant pastor Oskar Pfister that his works on religion were written to counter the destructive tendencies of religious institutions by inserting in their stead a veritable secular cure of souls (namely, psychoanalysis).[175] Freud thought that the latter would do what the "common-man's" religion could not: transform and educate the instincts in a manner that would create a more tolerant social whole.

It is further helpful to keep in mind that to a certain extent Freud's aim has been actualized. To wit: psychoanalytic theories and nomenclature have become a part of everyday life. One need only look at contemporary media outlets like movie screens, television, literature and social media to see that concepts like the unconscious, ego and superego have been part of our cultural soup. This empirical fact has led many theorists to describe modern Western culture as "therapeutic," as is well captured in W. H. Auden's '"Ode to Sigmund Freud" in which he framed Freud's impact on contemporary culture with the following words: "To us he is no more a person/Now, but a whole climate of opinion/Under whom we conduct our differing lives." The cultural soup we live in is so psychological that it is impossible to ignore the way in which it has influenced how we think about religion. As per our analysis, it is hardly unusual to think of religious narratives, myths and symbols as embodying, albeit in a disguised and transformed way, a host of developmental themes, anxieties and needs: "[t]here is a god for every psychic season, a myth for every hidden wish and a legend for every concealed anxiety."[176] Religious narratives are like

---

[175] See Freud's letter to Pfister of November 25, 1928, in H. Meng and E. L. Freud, eds., *Psychoanalysis and Faith*.

[176] S. Kakar, *Shamans, Mystics, Doctors*, p. 272.

"wearing the unconscious on the outside," being "cultural containers" for unconscious wishes and projections. Far from being a relic of the past, Freud's contribution to culture lives on. Indeed, properly applied, the intervention of psychoanalytic modes of analysis is a powerful tool in the disruption of the needless repetition of historical cycles that champion unpsychological institutions and their damaging doctrines.

References

Abel, E. (1990). Race, Class, and Psychoanalysis? Opening Questions. In M. Hirsch and E. F. Keller, eds., *Conflicts in Feminism*. New York: Routledge, 184–204.

Akhtar, S., ed. (2008). *The Crescent and the Couch*. New York: Jason Aronson.

Akhtar, S. and P. Tummala-Narra (2008). Psychoanalysis in India. In S. Akhtar, ed., *Freud along the Ganges*. New Delhi: Stanza, 3–28.

Albright, W. F. (1946). *From the Stone Age to Christianity*. Baltimore, MD: Johns Hopkins University Press.

Beit-Hallahmi, B. (2019). *Flesh and Blood: Interrogating Freud on Human Sacrifice, Real and Imagined*. Leiden: Brill.

Benslama, F. (2009). *Psychoanalysis and the Challenge of Islam*. Minneapolis: University of Minnesota Press.

Berger, P. (1990[1967]). *Sacred Canopy*. New York: Anchor Books. www .christiancentury.org/article/2012-03/protestantism-and-quest-certainty.

Bibring, E. (1941). The Development and Problems of the Theory of the Instincts. *International Journal of Psychoanalysis* 22, 102–131.

Brickman, C. (2003). *Aboriginal Populations in the Mind*. New York: Columbia University Press.

Chodorow, N. (1978). *The Reproduction of Mothering*. Berkeley: University of California Press.

Cooper, P. (2019). *Zen Insight, Psychoanalytic Action*. New York: Routledge.

Cooper-White, P. (2018). *Old and Dirty Gods: Religion, Antisemitism, and the Origins of Psychoanalysis*. New York: Routledge.

Douglas, M. (1982). The Effects of Modernization on Religious Change. In M. Douglas and S. Tipton, eds., *Religion and America: Spiritual Life in a Secular Age*. Boston, MA: Beacon Press, 25–43.

Drescher, E. (2016). *Choosing Our Religion: The Spiritual Lives of America's Nones*. New York: Oxford University Press.

Durkheim, E. (1965[1912]). *The Elementary Forms of the Religious Life*. New York: Free Press.

El Shakry, O. (2017). *The Arabic Freud*. Princeton, NJ: Princeton University Press.

Erikson, E. (1958). *Young Man Luther*. New York: W. W. Norton.

Fanon, F. (2008[1952]). *Black Skin, White Masks*. New York: Grove Press.

Freud, S. (1951). A Letter from Freud. *American Journal of Psychiatry* 107, 786–787.

(1966). *The Standard Edition of the Complete Psychological Works of Sigmund Freud* (S. E.). Volumes 1–24. Trans. and ed. J. Strachey. London: Hogarth Press.

Hamman, J. (2017). The Reproduction of the Hypermasculine Male: Select Subaltern Views. *Pastoral Psychology* 66, 799–818.

Hewitt, M. (2022). Review of "Freud and Religion: Advancing the Dialogue." By William B. Parsons. https://doi.org/10.1093/jaarel/lfac.038

James, W. (1929[1902]). *The Varieties of Religious Experience*. New York: Modern Library.

Jones, E. (1953–1957). *The Life and Work of Sigmund Freud*. 3 vols. New York: Basic Books.

Jones, J. (2008). *Blood That Cries Out from the Earth*. New York: Oxford University Press.

Jonte-Pace, D. (2001). Analysts, Critics, and Inclusivists: Feminist Voices in the Psychology of Religion. In D. Jonte-Pace and W. B. Parsons, eds., *Religion and Psychology: Mapping the Terrain*. New York: Routledge, 129–148.

(2006). Psychoanalysis, Colonialism, and Modernity: Reflections on Brickman's *Aboriginal Populations in the Mind. Religious Studies Review* 32(1), 1–4.

(2001). *Speaking the Unspeakable*. Berkeley: University of California Press.

Jung, C. (1977[1938]). *Psychology and Religion*. New Haven, CT: Yale University Press.

Kakar, S. (1991). The Guru As Healer. In S. Kakar, ed., *The Analyst and the Mystic*. Chicago, IL: University of Chicago Press, 35–54.

(1982). *Shamans, Mystics, Doctors*. New York: Alfred A. Knopf.

Kohut, H. (1978). Forms and Transformations of Narcissism. In P. Ornstein, ed., *The Search for the Self*. 2 vols. New York: International Universities Press, vol. 2: 427–460.

Kohut, H. and E. Wolf. (1978). The Disorders of the Self and Their Treatment: An Outline. *International Journal of Psychoanalysis* 59, 413–425.

Lacan, J. (1982). God and the Jouissance of Women. In J. Mitchell and J. Rose, eds., *Feminine Sexuality: Jacques Lacan and the Ecole Freudian*. New York: W. W. Norton, 137–149.

Lasch, C. (1979). *The Culture of Narcissism*. New York: W. W. Norton.

Lorand, J. (2018). *The Fetish Revisited: Marx, Freud, and the Gods Black People Make*. Durham, NC: Duke University Press.

Malinowski, B. (2012[1927]). *Sex and Repression in Savage Society*. London: Forgotten Books.

McCutcheon, R. (2018). *Studying Religion*. New York: Routledge.

McGrath, J. (1986). *Freud's Discovery of Psychoanalysis: The Politics of Hysteria*. Ithaca, NY: Cornell University Press.

Meissner, W. W. (1986). *Psychoanalysis and Religious Experience*. New Haven, CT: Yale University Press.

Meng, H. and E. L. Freud, eds. (1963). *Psychoanalysis and Faith: The Letters of Sigmund Freud and Oskar Pfister*. New York: Basic Books.

Miller, C. and N. Carlin. (2010). Joel Osteen As Cultural Self-Object: Meeting the Needs of the Group Self and Its Individual Members in and from the Largest Church in America. *Pastoral Psychology* 59, 27–51.

Mitchell, J. (2000[1974]). *Psychoanalysis and Feminism*. New York: Basic Books.

Obeyesekere, G. (1990). *The Work of Culture*. Chicago, IL: University of Chicago Press.

Parsons, W. B., ed. (2018). *Being Spiritual but Not Religious: Past, Present, Future(s)*. New York: Routledge.

 (1999). *The Enigma of the Oceanic Feeling*. New York: Oxford University Press.

 (2013). *Freud and Augustine in Dialogue*. Charlottesville: University of Virginia Press.

 (2021). *Freud and Religion: Advancing the Dialogue*. Cambridge: Cambridge University Press.

Pfister, O. (1993). The Illusion of the Future: A Friendly Disagreement with Prof. Sigmund Freud. *International Journal of Psychoanalysis* 74, 557–579.

Rice, E. (1990). *Freud and Moses*. Albany: State University of New York Press.

Rizzuto, A. (1979). *The Birth of the Living God*. Chicago, IL: University of Chicago Press.

Said, E. (2003). *Freud and the Non-European*. New York: Verso.

Schorske, C. (1981). *Fin-de-Siècle Vienna*. New York: Vintage.

Smith, J. Z. (1988). *Imagining Religion*. Chicago, IL: University of Chicago Press.

Smith, W. C. (1991[1962]). *The Meaning and End of Religion*. Minneapolis, MN: Fortress Press.

Thatamanil, J. J. (2020). *Circling the Elephant: A Comparative Theory of Religious Diversity*. New York: Fordham University Press.

Wallace, E. (1983). *Freud and Anthropology*. New York: International Universities Press.

Wallwork, E. (1991). *Psychoanalysis and Ethics*. New Haven, CT: Yale University Press.

Webb, R. and M. Sells (1995). Lacan and Bion: Psychoanalysis and the Mystical Language of Unsaying. *Theory and Psychology* 5(2), 195–215.

Winnicott, D. W. (1971). *Playing and Reality.* New York: Penguin.

Wolfson, E. (1997). *Through a Speculum That Shines.* Princeton, NJ: Princeton University Press.

Yerushalmi, Y. H. (1991). *Freud's Moses: Judaism Terminable and Interminable.* New Haven, CT: Yale University Press.

Cambridge Elements $\equiv$

Religion and Monotheism

Chad Meister

Bethel University

Chad Meister is Professor of Philosophy and Theology and Department Chair at Bethel College. He is the author of *Introducing Philosophy of Religion* (Routledge, 2009), *Christian Thought: A Historical Introduction*, 2nd edition (Routledge, 2017), and *Evil: A Guide for the Perplexed*, 2nd edition (Bloomsbury, 2018). He has edited or co-edited the following: *The Oxford Handbook of Religious Diversity* (Oxford University Press, 2010), *Debating Christian Theism* (Oxford University Press, 2011), with Paul Moser, *The Cambridge Companion to the Problem of Evil* (Cambridge University Press, 2017), and with Charles Taliaferro, *The History of Evil* (Routledge 2018, in six volumes).

Paul K. Moser

Loyola University Chicago

Paul K. Moser is Professor of Philosophy at Loyola University Chicago. He is the author of *Understanding Religious Experience, The God Relationship, The Elusive God* (winner of national book award from the Jesuit Honor Society), *The Evidence for God, The Severity of God, Knowledge and Evidence* (all Cambridge University Press), and *Philosophy after Objectivity* (Oxford University Press); co-author of *Theory of Knowledge* (Oxford University Press); editor of *Jesus and Philosophy* (Cambridge University Press) and *The Oxford Handbook of Epistemology* (Oxford University Press); and co-editor of *The Wisdom of the Christian Faith* (Cambridge University Press). He is the co-editor with Chad Meister of the book series Cambridge Studies in Religion, Philosophy, and Society.

About the Series

This Cambridge Element series publishes original concise volumes on monotheism and its significance. Monotheism has occupied inquirers since the time of the Biblical patriarch, and it continues to attract interdisciplinary academic work today. Engaging, current, and concise, the Elements benefit teachers, researchers, and advanced students in religious studies, Biblical studies, theology, philosophy of religion, and related fields.

Cambridge Elements ≡

Religion and Monotheism

Elements in the Series

A full series listing is available at: www.cambridge.org/er&m